AF731320

COMMERCE AND INFORMATION TECHNOLOGY

COMMERCE AND INFORMATION TECHNOLOGY

A. VINAYAGAMOORTHY

SERIALS PUBLICATIONS
NEW DELHI

© A. Vinayagamoorthy

First Published - 2007

ISBN : 81-8387-072-4

All rights reservedwith the Publisher, including the right to translate or reproduce this book or parts thereof except for brief quotations in critical articles or reviews.

Published by

SERIALS PUBLICATIONS
4830/24, Prahlad Street, Ansari Road
Darya Ganj, New Delhi-110002 (India)
Phone : 23245225. Fax : 91-11-23272135
E-mail: serials@satyam.net.in

CONTENTS

PART - V : Agriculture

PART - VI : Co-operation

PART - VII : General

FELICITATION

It gives me immense pleasure that Dr. A. Vinayagamoorthy, Reader in Commerce, Periyar University, Salem-636 011, is brining out his papers, published in various journals–Indian and Foreign in the form of a book, entitled "Twinkling Thirty-Commerce and Information Technology" (Collection of Research Papers in Commerce and Related Subjects). The papers, included in this book, provide broader insight and deeper analysis of various current topics. The concepts, theories and techniques used in these papers are very simple and written in a transparent, plain and easily understandable language. The papers are arranged and grouped under various titles in a sequential manner and a reader would find it like a flow. The book will be of great help to academician, research scholars, executives and students.

I know, this book is one more feather to his cap.

I wish him all success in all his future endeavour

Sacred Heart College
Tirupattur – 635 601

Dr. K. Padmanabhan
Professor and Head (Retd.)
Department of Economics

FELICITATION

I have great pleasure to know that Dr. A. Vinauyagamoorthy, Reader in Commerce, Periyar University, Salem–636 011is publishing a book entitled "Twinkling Thirty-Commerce and Information Technology" {Collection of Research Papers in Commerce and Related Subjects} which contains 30 research papers published by him in leading journals both in India and abroad on various occasions.

This book provides a penetrating and comprehensive analysis of the concepts, theories and techniques in a simple, lucid, unambiguous and precise manner. I am quite confident that this book will greatly help the academics, research scholars, financial executives, bankers and students.

I wish him every success in all his future endeavour.

Vellore –632 006

Mr. V. Jayaraman, IFS, (Retd.)
Chief Conservator of Forest
Govt. of India

FELICITATION

I have great pleasure to know that Dr. A. Vinayagamoorthy, Reader in Commerce, Periyar University, Salem-636011 is publishing a book entitled "twinkling Thirty-Commerce and Information Technology" which contains 30 research papers published by him in leading journals both in India and abroad on various occasions.

This book provides a penetrating and comprehensive analysis of the concepts, theories and techniques in a simple, lucid, unambiguous and precise manner. I am quite confident that this book will be of great help to the academics, research scholars, financial executives, Bankers, Insures and students.

I wish him every success in all his future endeavours.

Periyar University
Salem-636011

Prof. Dr. T. Balakrishnan
Vice-Chancellor

FOREWORD

Commerce encompasses a wide range of subjects such as Marketing, Agriculture, Taxation, Insurance, Financial services, etc. This book is an attempt to compile the Research Papers the authour has worked on such varied subjects.

The book contains 30 papers of the authour, out of which 4 each are in Global Business, Agriculture, and Insurance, 3 in Marketing and 2 each are in Taxation and Co-operation and the remaining can be classified under General. The General category includes 'Papers in Mutual Fund, ' Information Technology and E-Commerce', ' Tribal Welfare and 'Tourism'. Though these papers cover specific areas of Commerce they have been included in the General Category because there is only one paper.

The four papers in Global Business explain four of the various dimensions of Global Business such as BPO, GATS and banking, Accounting and Banking. BPO is the current trend in Global business. India is a preferred destination for BPO. The benefits of BPO to both the host and the contracting countries have been lucidly explained. A wide range of 'E' banking services, their benefits, problems in their application and suggestions for better use have been exhaustively dealt with.

The four papers in Agriculture are exceptional in the sense that they deal with certain trends, which are normally missed or skipped over by the Researchers in Agriculture. The writer has established Agriculture is not a losing proposition, citing an example. He has enlisted a wealth of information and opportunities to youngsters for their service in forestry. The present position and problems of landless labour are discussed in detail in another paper. The suggestions are worthy of serious consideration for implementation by the powers that be. The importance of trees in environment protection etc., have been brought to limelight in the paper "Grow More Trees".

Insurance is a fertile and unexplored area in Commerce. Especially after LPG, Private Sector has entered the field and enhanced the competition to the public sector. But the literature in this subject is very limited. The author has written four papers in Insurance. He has highlighted the need for insurance in rural areas. He has also brought out the fact that the entry of Private Sector has contributed to the benefit of the insured in terms of product innovation, customer education and services, and Marketing Strategies. The need for new marketing strategies and Modern Marketing approach has also been emphasized.

The three papers on Marketing are on different notes. The first paper, Purchase Decision and Consumer Behaviour is a good research work enlisting the steps in decision making process in making purchases of durable goods. The other two papers Marketing of Leather Products and Consumers View on Petrol Prices are more informative.

The two papers on taxation, Service Tax and VAT are valuable contributions from the author on current trends in the subjects. All the advantages of VAT have been highlighted. The author has taken pains to explain VAT is advantageous to all concerned. Many of the advantages were not brought to light before by any other researcher. Another two papers on Co-operation, Performance of Industrial Co-operative societies in Tamil Nadu-recent Trends and Women Empowerment through Co-operative Societies are valuable contributions from the author on current trends in the subjects.

The subjects in which one paper has been produced and a few general subjects have been classified under General category. There is one paper each in Tourism, Tribal Welfare, Women Entrepreneurship, Information Technology and 'E' Commerce and Mutual Fund. These papers are highly informative. The paper in Commerce Education brings out the need for changes in commerce curriculum. The statement "Commerce education becomes an education for better living" sums up the objective of commerce education and suitable changes should be implemented accordingly. The paper on "All India Services–Past, Present and Future" provides a wealth of information to candidates aspiring for such services.

The case studies explained in "Secret of Success" and "Railway Pioneering Institute" provide role models of individuals and institutions.

The book contains the industry and hard work put in by the author over a few years. It bears testimony to his expertise on varied subjects of commerce and related areas. Such a collection of papers on a wide range of subjects is rare. Thus this work can serve as a good reference material for students, Teachers and Research Scholars in Commerce and related areas.

My hearty congratulations to the author and best wishes.

S. SHANMUGASUNDARAM

ACKNOWLEDGEMENTS

In Planning and completing this book, I have drawn help fro0m various sources and wishes to acknowledge them with a sense of gratitude and appreciation.

It is with all the sincerity at my command and from the deepest abyss of my heart, I express my thanks to those connected with the successful completion of the book. Among the large number of individual, one person stands out and that is my guide Dr. K. Padmanabhan, Head and Professor of Economic, Sacred Heart college, (Autonomous), Tirupattur-635 601. Vellore District, Tamil Nadu. His editorial comments were always to the point and his generous and spirited guidance helped me to pull the work to final completion.

Dr. S. Shanmugasundaram, Professor and Head, Department of Commerce, Periyar University, Salem–636011, has extended his helping hand kindly and generously to me in more ways than one in the preparation and completion of the book. Words fail me when I try to thank him. He was totally responsible in the correction of manuscripts. His motto, 'Systematic Perseverance', yields right results and has worked well on a number of occasions. I doubt if I can ever repay my debt of gratitude I owe him. My sincere gratitude is due to Dr. S. Shanmugasundaram, for his kindness in writing the foreword for this book.

I extend my sincere thanks to Prof. Dr. V. Balakrishnan, Vice Chancellor, Periyar University, Salem–636011 who provided me timely guidance and encouragement. I owe a deep debt of gratitude to Dr. G. Kunasekaran, Registrar i/c, Periyar University, Salem – 636 011 for all his guidance and support.

My special thanks to my colleagues Dr. A. Jayakumar, Reader Dr. K. Maruthamuthu, Dr. K. Prabhakar Rajkumar, Mr. K. Krishna Kumar, Dr. M. Sumathy, Lecturers Department of Commerce Periyar

University, Salem – 636 011 for their appreciation and earnest support given to me in publishing this book.

I owe a deep sense of gratitude to my mentor Mr. V. Jayaraan, IFS, Chief Conservator of Forest (Retd.) Govt. of India, as it was he who groomed me to set my sight on this book of academic excellence.

My special thanks to Mr. R. Gopi, Mr. M. Chithirai Selvan, Lecturers, NGM College, Pollachi, Ms. K. R. Vijaysanthi and R. Sathya M. Phil. Research Scholars and Ms. C. Nagalakshmi, Mr. T. Thirupathi, C.U. Sampath, Ph.D. Research Scholars.

My sincere thanks are due to Prof. V. Rahmatulla, Lecturer, Department of English, Islamiah College, Vaniyambadi, and Mrs. S. Amutha, Lecturer, Department of English, M.K. Jain College, Vaniyambadi, for his and her great help from the beginning till the end of the study.

My sincere thanks are due to Dr. M. Manickam, Professor and Head, Department of Commerce, Dr. S. Sudalaimuthu, and Dr. P. Chellasamy, Lecturers, Department of Commerce, Bharathiar University, Coimbatore for their great help from the beginning till the end of the study.

I sincerely thank the Proprietor of TCDS Computer Center at Jolarpettai, Advocate A. Gnanamohan, M.Com., M.Phil., LLB., for the neat execution of the text through MS Word Processing.

I sincerely thank the Management of Sacred Heart College, Particularly Rev. Fr. Dr. Varghees, SDB, Principal, Fr. Maria Soosai, SDB, Vice-Principal (Evening College) who helped me in all possible ways to complete my book.

My wife, N. Sengani, M.Com., M.Phil., B.Ed., who has been a source of inspiration, deserves a word of thanks. My beloved daughter Ms. V. Vaishali, and my son Mr. V. Vignesh helped me by the supply of pencil, eraser etc., during my correction work. My thanks are due to each one of them.

A final word of thanks to the designers, Printers Publications, Serials Publications, New Delhi for bringing out this book neatly and successfully within a short time.

Finally and most importantly, many thanks to my parents for their affectionate blessings and loving co-operation at all moments of this academic venture. To them, I will be forever grateful. The process of learning continues.

A. Vinayagamoorthy

Ever grateful
To
My Parents
Late Mr. K. Anumuthan
And
Mrs. Rajammal Anumuthan

Dedicated to the Revered Thirumigu Kalvithanthai K. M. Govindarajanar, Chairman, KMG Group of Institutions, Gudiyattam. He is 87 years old freedom fighter and going tough in following Gandhian principles even at this age. He is a complete man in every aspect in Gudiyattam town. He is a successful industrialist, educationalist and a social worker. He is a man of courage, hard work and integrity. He served much of his life for the independence of our country.

PART - I
GLOBAL BUSINESS

ACCOUNTING FOR GLOBALISATION AND ITS IMPACT ON CORPORATE REPORTING

Introduction

Accounting is often called the language of business. The basic function of any language is to serve as a means of communication. The financial result of different companies cannot be compared and evaluated unless full information is available about the accounting methods, which have been used. The varieties of accounting practices have made it difficult to compare the financial result of different companies. Further, the alternative accounting methods have also enabled the reporting of different result even by the same company.

Need for Standards

The information contained in published financial statement is of particular important to external user; it is the responsibility of the accounting profession to ensure that the required information is property presented. The information contained in financial s statement to carefully considered standards. In this context, unless there are reasonably appropriate standards, neither the purpose of the individual investor nor that of the nation as a whole can be served. The purpose is likely to be served if the accounting methods used by different firms for presenting information to investor allows correct compression to be made.

Changing Nature of Generally Accepted Accounting Principles (GAAP)

GAAP are usually developed by professional accounting bodies like Americans institute of certified public accounting and institute of chartered accountants of India. In developing such principles, however, the accounting profession has to reflect the realities of social, economic, legal and political environment in which it operates. Besides academic research, regulatory and tax laws of the government in a large measure, influences the formulation of acceptable accounting principles. Stock exchange and other regulatory agencies like controller of capital issues have laid down rules for disclosure and extent of accounting information. Since the environment in which business operated undergoes constant changes as a result of changes in economic and financial policies of the government and changes in the structure of business, continued evaluation of the revenue of generally accounting principle is required. In this, the principal of accounting are not everlasting truths.

Accounting for Global Business

Recent years have witnessed the growth of global environment influences upon business activities of the MNCs. Different economic, legal, social, political dimension have opened a new horizon of international business and simultaneously have been changed on account of change in technologies rebated with information, communication, space, computer and so on, especially in the last decade to the 20th century, therefore, changes in accounting become mandatory. The global business entrusted new challenges and responsibilities upon the accounting professionals, professors, personnel and bodies to fit accounting to the changes business environment of the world as a whole.

The GATT also encouraged the global in whom business in which 124 countries signed to primate world trade in a manner that benefits every country in its 8th round meting held at Uruguay (south America) on aprial 15, 1994.

Accounting and Foreign Transactions

The role of accountant increase as on enterprise engages in foreign trades. Accounting has to deal with monetary mechanism and other transactions related to the international business.

Globalize international business having multinational companies by virtue of nature required of special and standardized system of accounting. As the international business covers a range of actives, accounting must be in accordance with the need of such transactions which may be recorded reported and analyzed for decision making by the internal and external user. Accounting has to serve the need of international trade, commerce, industry, international finance, taxation, currency, export-import procedures, documentations laws, trade – environment, auditing etc.

The global business required such as a system of accounting in which no scope for personal biasness and it should be automatic, irrupted, and transparent system involving a greater sense of self responsibility interest, loyalty, integrity and honesty.

Beside computer accounting, accounting language there are a number of other voices related with accounting for MNCs in global business such as forms preformed of final account foot-notes schedules, statement etc have their due consideration.

Changing Horizon of the Accounting Practices

The changes that are taking place in the different facets of traditional accounting practices in the global accounting scenario are given below:

	Past Scenario	Present Scenario
1.	Profitability performance accounting	Total performance accounting
2.	Unit cost accounting	Unit value accounting
3.	Product costing-	Services accounting
4.	Overhead absorption costing	Activity based costing
5.	Depreciation accounting	Appreciation accounting
6.	HR as expense accounting	HR as asset accounting
7.	2:1 Liquidity accounting	Zero liquidity accounting
8.	Debtors velocity accounting	Customer as asset accounting
9.	Creditors velocity accounting	Suppliers as asset accounting
10.	Environment protection expense accounting	Greenhouse accounting
11.	Goodwill writer off accounting	Goodwill as asset accounting
12.	Standard cost of mass production	Elemental cost under flexible manufacturing system
13.	Extrapolation as budgeting	Zero base budgeting
14.	Expenditure budgeting-	Performance budgeting
15.	Historical cost accounting	Relevant cost accounting
16.	Historical cost accounting	On-line cost control
17.	Owned asset accounting	Not-owned asset accounting
18.	Statutory audit	Operation/energy/quality/ management audit
19.	Money flow accounting	Real flow accounting
20.	National accounting standards	International accounting standards.

From the table, it is apparent that the traditional accounting practices are going through the process of transformation to meet the ever-increasing demands of supporitiverole of accounting in different function Ares of corporate management.

Accounting Standards in India

With a view to harmonies varying accounting policies and practices currently in use in India, the institute of chartered accountant of India (ICAI) formed the accounting standards board, (ASB) April 1977, which includes representatives from industry and government. So far 10 standards have been issued by ASB.

Attempts Towads Standardisation

International accounting standards committee was formed and was entrusted with the responsibility of formulating international standards. All the member countries of IASC resolved to confirm to the standards developed by IASC. Attempts have also been made in countries of European Economic Community and Canada for sanitation of accounting practices regarding disclosure and consistency of procedures.

Gloobalisatuion-it's Consequences to Indian Corporate Reporting

The following are certain critical areas of the Indian corporate accounting to be corrected and reported with international accounts standards.

Group Accounting

International standards prescribe consolidation for subsidiaries; equity method for associated and proportion consolidation for equity joint ventures in India the approach followed does not provide full information determining the efficiency and effectiveness of thaw management.

Business Cobinations

India has accounting rules in place, only to deal with legal merged and not with other modes of combination. Internationally, the process of uniting interest is treated as an exception on account of the potential that exists for manipulation the EPS of the combined entity. Indian accounting rule provide scope for creative accounting.

Foreign Activities

Indian accounting rules in respect of foreign activities are divergent from the international standards in the following crucial areas.

(a) All exchange differences are required to be reorganized and the exchange losses can be amortized. The Indian rules are liberal whereas the international standards are stringent and logical.

(b) Indian rules do not make any distinction between independent and integral foreign operations.

Profit or Loss for the Period

In order to enable intra-firm and inter-firm comparison of earning, the international standards requires corporate to give full and comprehensive information on the effect of fundamental errors, unordinary items and changes in accounting policy contrarily, Indian accounting rules appear tentative incomplete in these areas.

EPS

At present there is no uniformity in the method of computing EPS. Consequently the EPS data presentation is misleading and unhelpful for analysis. There is a need to create standards on the computation of EPS in line with the IAS.

Others

1. Furnishing Information on Industry and Geographical Segments.
2. Tribulation norms in clear cut terms for measuring and disclosing current assets and current liabilities.
3. Providing information on sales, cost value of goods sold and gross profit.
4. Presenting cash flow statements.
5. Interim reporting.

Conclusion

Us and international accounting practices vary significantly. Worldwide accounting uniformity is an unattainable goal. This due to differences in economic, political and social values, and in the different developments I, and goals of each individual country. However, IASC and the IOSCO were formed to promote same kind of accounting uniformity throughout the world.

BUSINESS PROCESS OUTSOURCING

Is India shinning? Like the farmers in a village to know the market trend from their village itself; married girls to inform their parents the situation in their in-laws place; Government departments to celebrate their achievements at convenient point of time.

In all these, the concept of India shinning depends upon how one views, but in one aspect all agree without any controversy that India shines is in BPO. In BPO all countries wonder that India is shinning, BPO is much talked about among unemployed youth. "India is a center for BPO" is the talk of the world. Most countries prefer India for BPO. Unemployed youth are groomed for BPO. BPO is the only source of employment for the unemployed, since Govt. jobs are almost nil. BPO is the only resort now and also in future for youngsters.

What is BPO?

BPO is the act of giving to a third-party sundry works (other than the core works) at a less remunerative rate. The firm does the core works itself, which is unavoidable though costly. For instance, an insurance company might outsource their "Claims process " and scriptary works or a bank might out source their loan processing system.

Companies that are looking at business process outsourcing are hoping to achieve cost savings by giving away sundry works to a third party; which party can take advantage of this and by doing the same work for many companies due to less labour costs make out their livelihood.

Benefits of BPO

BPO is way to improve operational performance of any firm simultaneously building up economy of developing countries. India is the dominant location for foot-wears and shoes services due to its massive pool of low-cost labour.

A big firm, concern, institution, establishment wants not to spend money on sundry works. These are given to economically poor countries so that not much money and energy is spent. Else comparatively more money had to be spent on this indirect items. In the recent past Britain, America is resorting to this, resulting India, growing 300% on BPO. By 2006, the employees on BPO in India may cross 4 lakhs, with an earning of 1,200/- of dollars.

BPO refers to decision to sub-contract some or all non-core processes.

The main motive for BPO is to allow the company to invest more time, money and human resources into core active items without losing quality and name.

BPO [Business Process Outsourcing] has been the latest mantra in India now a days.

As the current sources of revenue face slower growth, software companies are trying new ways to increase their revenues.

BPO is top on their list Today

India has one of the largest pool of low-cost English speaking scientific and technical talent. This makes India one obvious choice to out source Dell, Sun Microsystems, LG, Ford, GE, Oracle all have announced plans to scale up their operations in India.

Many call centers have come up in India serving several foreign airlines and banks in BPO.

Many European and Us companies have realized that they should focus on their main business and outsource their Human Resource Department, and accounting department etc., to BPO.

BPO saves precious management time and resources and allows focus while building upon core competencies.

BPO is one way of increasing their profits. BPO results in increasing shareholder value too.

If a bank shifts work of a 1000 people from US to India it can save about $18 million a year due to lower cost in India.

Other Benefits

- Productivity Improvements
- Access to expertise
- Operational cost control
- Cost savings
- Improved accountability
- Improved HR
- Opportunity to focus on core business

It gives a clear cost advantage to the company that is giving out the work. The main advantage is cost saving. Out sourcing helps convert a fixed cost structures to a variable one and allows for more flexibility to handle the uncertainties of business.

Benefits of BPO to other countries

Other countries are not for keeping permanent labour for miscellaneous items. These countries get their jobs done by giving away these sundry items as BPO. 'Directly involving items' and in higher positions their natives are employed with extra remuneration. By shirking the Sundry items, these big firms can concentrate on core items and be successful.

The persons taking to BPO start with Rs.5000/= as pay which goes upto Rs.50, 000/= in due course. In view of the prevalence of unemployment the opportunity by BPO and the remuneration from it is a boon to our country.

Other countries have to shell out many times compared to our country to get the same work done. In the present day in view of the competitive market, unless expenditure is brought down other countries may not be able to flourish. BPO is the only hope.

Answering customers; recording to compliance of call centers; listening to doctors or listening to audio cassettes; in preparing medical transcriptions; maintaining insurance account; setting up computer centers; preparing software's; graphics; animation; multimedia; scanning are the avenues in BPO.

Fluent conversing, in attracting other countries (e.g. Americans or Britain's) is a sure way of getting employment. Youngsters adept in this and who can finish their assignments to the other countries are called "BPO vendors."

Britishers by dialing a particular number can get to know the railway timings and such other needs where in the other side are the BPO vendors.

Recently, 100 million pound sterling has been given to our country by the Britain railway establishment through BPO. Everyday on a average 1,50,000/- require railway details. Out of these, 50% can be answered by unemployed Indians through BPO. In the past two years, Americans had allotted computer, medical transcriptions. Dialogues are going on in such other matters by foreign companies. BPO is a hotly discussed subject now without which proportionate job opportunities will be lost.

Politically also: BPO is one of the election issues in American presidential poll. John Kerry, the presidential candidates of Republican Party is much vociferous against

BPO stating that it is making in roads into their economy. The job opportunity for their natives getting reduced by BPO. They accuse that the BPO supporters are Benefits Arnold groups.

Benefit Arnold took to British side in the American liberal fights. In short John Kerry accuses benefit Arnold and such minded persons are traitors of America. The American central Govt. is planning to discuss about banning of BPO. Efforts are on in 20 states to put an end to BPO. It is felt that President Bush may find it going tough in the elections on account of BPO. But the recent information establishes that the American firms are for BPO.

It is curious to know that a double standard is adopted by America viz; one side it advocates that there should be no control in the world trade and all obstacles in the way to be removed and these should be free trades. on the other side efforts are to bring in legislation for abolishing BPO. This is voiced by not less than our previous deputy Prime Minister L.K. Advani.

Even the America based Indians feel that they may thrown out of employment if BPO continuous. This looks like Indians usurping employment of Americans. But this should be viewed in the perspective of India is helping them in getting over rival traders. Efforts should be made to remove this misapprehension says NR Narayanamoorthy Interpol leader. In 20 states, 60 proposals have been accepted in America against BPO.

The CIA has examined as to how BPO will cut in economy and security of America. Country that created global citizens is trying to safe guard locals with a disturbed mood. BPO established that unless the third world countries give their help, developed countries may not be able to keep up their position. In the recently held WTO, India proved the resources of the third world countries. Again through BPO, this is established "India shines".

GATS AND ITS IMPACT ON BANKING SERVICES IN INDIA

Introduction

Trade in services runs into trillions of dollars each year and in some developed countries. It accounts for over 60% of their GNP. The objective of the General Agreement on Trade and Services (GATS) is to promote economic growth of all trading partners through the expansion of trade in services, under conditions of transparency and progressive liberalization.

The impact of GATS on Banking Services would be multi-dimensional leading to changes in:

1. The structure and functions of Banking system
2. The Banking policy, programmes and its implementation
3. The role of regulatory bodies
4. Individual Institutional policy
5. The Acts and Statutes of Banking and RBI Acts

India, being a signatory of WTO and GATS has to open necessarily its door and abide by the conditions and laws of GATS. Article-1 of GATS defines four modes of supply in any service including Banking service.

Banking sector is an important cornerstone to our economy. Global integration of financial markets resulted from de-regulating measures, technological explosion and financial innovations. With the entry of private and foreign players in the Banking business, people have got a host of options to choose from.

WTO deserves that the customers must receive different banking services that would benefit him as well as the society in time.

Moreover, it supports the globalisation, which enables the customer to choose independently among the various services offered by the global players. Thereby, it secures the interest of the customers. The healthy competition in the sector enabled the giant Banker of our mother country.

The banking sector is in a transitional mode towards a vibrant global market and sophisticated information technology. Due to this changing scenario, banks are paying more attention to expanding their activities from just lending and borrowing to other ends like, insurance merchant banking, leasing, electronic banking etc. Even though these changes were expected after the nationalization of banks in 1969, it was noticed that it had only slow and steady progress necessitating a total revamping of the banking sector. Various reform measures were taken to strengthen the foundation of the system by improving asset quality, enhancing capital and improving profitability along with structural changes in the system. During this transition, banks have seen fierce competition, risk, and revolutionary changes forcing them to take immediate steps to retain market share, redress the grievances of customers as fast as possible buy maintaining good ambience, rendering courteous services to customers with the help of latest technological innovations and products.

Globalization and liberalization have forced the banks to think in terms of technology benefits and quality service to customers as future is full of challenges and survival will be a difficult task. The entry of IT infrastructure in the corporate world of banks has brought with it many innovations, in particular the Internet. Though these changes had started with Narasimham Committee's (1992) suggestions for computerization and were followed by Saraf Committee's (1994) recommendations for electronic fund transfers (EFT), Electronic Clearing Services (ECS) and automatic data capture, the banks were actually required to use the BANKET and RBINET and Internet to accommodate itself to the innumerous transactions that had resulted as a result of globalization and liberalization.

The Indian banking industry is not lagging behind, it has started providing services electronically over the internet. These services rendered over electronic media include:

- Phone banking
- ATM–Automatic Teller Machines
- Credit Cards
- Electronic Fund Transfer –EFT
- Shared Payment Network System – SPNS
- Electronic Clearing Service - ECS
- Point of Sale – POS
- D-Mat Accounts
- Electronic Data Interchange
- E-Cheques
- Corporate Banking Terminal

E-Banking Services

These services provided by using electronic technology and media are called information technology or electronic banking or e-banking. E-banking has given an opportunity for banks to find solutions to management problems like saving time money and energy or customers by reducing/minimising paper works, waiting in queues, lack of communication and lack of efficiency. E-banking has provided ease and flexibility in banking operations. The recommendations of Narashimham Committee (1998), for the free and liberal entry of foreign banks in India have further improved the scope for e-banking. As many foreign banks and private sector banks like CITI Bank and ICICI, HDFC banks brought with them IT based products like ATM, credit cards, debit cards, on-line banking etc. This forced the public sector banks and other banks to think on the same lines as these services would help banks to retain their customers, target on banking products and services more effectively to customers.

Customers are also benefited as they are given more free time to indulge in e-commerce business. Therefore, after 1980 throughout the world with majority of banking transactions done through nets or by using information technology. So the information technology solves many problems of the banking industry and very useful to the customers too.

Application of E-Banking Services

Phone Banking

Bank on phone, provides easy access for customers to have large businesses through telephones. Data are exchanged over the phone regarding any queries, to issue instructions on balance transfer, statement of account, cheque book, stop payments, new schemes, interest rates etc. at any convenient time and place. Telebanking has gone a long way in providing maximum customer satisfaction within the limited infrastructure.

Automatic Teller Machines: (ATM)

Banks in the cities to provide cash dispensation to their customers around the clock install ATMs. Now, the banks provide this facility in a more sophisticated way that a customer of one bank and branch can withdraw from any other banks, at any other branch, nation wide. In developed countries, this service is provided to their blue chip client globally. This is possible only through worldwide networking and communication system.

Credit Cards

These plastic cards enable customers to spend whenever he/ she wants within the prescribed limits and pay later. Debit cards is a prepaid card with stored value, whereas credit card is post paid with fixed limits. It is seen that spending is higher through debit cards than with credit cards currently CITY Bank and time bank have started with Debit cards and now other banks are also following these to launch their own cards.

Electronic Funds Transfer: (EFT)

Electronic funds transfer is a system of processing and communication of payment through el4ectronic methods. EFT assumes greater significance in the banking system as the RBI also encourages the commercial banks to adopt this technique. Inter and intra bank transfers of funds are now made through this EFT mechanism. Transactions of high value i.e., at least more than one lakh is now made through this cost effective and quick system of settlement. Normally, payments are made through cash, cheques, drafts and credit cards. The latest in this process are the debit card system, charge, digital cash, electronic purse and so on.

SPNS- Shared Payment Network System

SPNS installed by the IBA in the city of Mumbai, enables electronic banking service like cash transactions, extended hours of banking, utility payments, cheques, point of sale facilities by the SPNS can go to any ATM linked to SPNS.

Electronic Clearing Services [ECS]

Electronic clearing of funds from one centre to another for handling bulk transactions like salary, interest, dividend, commission etc., has dispensed the cheques. A part of electronic clearing service is computerized clearing of cheques at metropolitan centers and linking with international communication system of SWIFT. These services have contributed in a great way towards improving the customer services globally. ECS was introduced in India in 1996. It has made it possible for customers to get the funds next day itself.

Point of Sale [POS] Terminal

Payment card at a retail location for electronic transfer of fund is called POS. The client enters his personal identification number [PIN] and confirms the amount due. Customer's account is automatically debited with the amount of purchases and it credits the retailers account POS installed at petrol stations and large retail houses are linked to banks network.

D-Mat Accounts

Transacting shares business through electronic media is called D-Mat. Investor opens an account called Demat Accounts with DPS. They get shares in electronic form.. Then they send the actual shares to the investor. Investor pays for the opening, maintenance and collection of shares. This has reduced the paper work, bad deliveries; loss of shares and less transaction cost. However delays in demating, higher cost charged by the investors has not given a good start for the growth and scope of Demat in India. Depository participant sometimes make illegal money at the cost of investors. SEBI should find ways to over come this to give a good scope for Demat in India.

Electronic Data Interchange-EDI

EDI refers to the electronic exchange of structure information using telecommunication like payment orders, debits credits, statement of account etc. As part of EDI, satellite communication network is also entering the banks. EDI will very soon do away with branch banking and the customers will identified as ban customer and not branch customer.

E-cheques

Digital cheque used by the payer to the payee through internet is called e-cheques. Electronic versions of cheques are issued, received and processed. Most of the banks use e-cheques. A secure means of operation is provided for collecting, payments, and transferring cash flows through this method. The payer issues a digital cheque to the payee and the entire transactions are done through internet.

Corporate Banking Terminal

Logging to banks database and assessing their accounts and transactions is a part of large corporate customers abroad. In India, so far the banks have not leashed into this venture.

RBI Net: (RBI NET)

This scheme facilitates the transfer of funds by a customer former any bank, any branch, any center to his client at some other center, so other bank and/or branch. Settlements between banks and with the RBI are now a day done through this system. Inter and Intra bank clearing are also done through this electronic communication system.

The following are the specific Areas where information technology can be used in the banking system:

(i) Preparation and posting in ledger (LAN)
(ii) Portfolio management (genetic algorithm)
(iii) Funds management and transfer (on-line banking)
(iv) Credit appraisal
(v) Foreign exchange transaction
(vi) Opening of letter of credit
(vii) Issue of letter of guarantee
(viii) Decision making at senior manager level
(ix) Employees training and education
(x) Preparation and submission of financial statements

(xi) Identification of fraudulent credit card transactions (neutral network system).

Benefits

The information technology can be administered in the banking system. The application of information technology will help in increasing the operating efficiency of the banking system. Its application will result in saving in cost. The quality of the information can be improved. The branches can provide improved customer services. This will enable the domestic banks to face and challenge the competition from their foreign rivals. There will be a reduction in the staff strength to a considerable extent due to the adoption of information technology. The working condition of the bank branches can be improved.

Benefits of E-Banking Services

- It reduces cost of both in services and administration.
- Overcoming the geographhical barriers.
- Cost minimized for customers.
- It helps to maintain customer loyalty.
- Web site enable banks to develop advertisement.
- Information technology enable banks to deliver products and services .
- Multimedia capabilities offer homogenous branding.
- Online banking encourages promotion of various schemes of the bank.
- Individualised and customized services with the help of integrated customer data.
- Minimising fraud and misappropriation by inter-branch reconciliation.
- Convenience to customers–like card free banking, cash free banking provides a domain of access to banking services.

Reasons for Poor Achievement

1. Poor initial introduction of the information technology concepts in the banks.
2. Improper implementation of techniques of information technology.
3. Improper selection of hardware and software will result in heavy cost and inefficiency.
4. Inadequate suppliers support after the purchase of the IT system.
5. Fear and reluctance among the staff regarding reduction of staff followed by retrenchment due to the introduction of information technology.
6. Brain drain is yet another cause for the poor implementation of the information technology.
7. Lack of co-ordination between the management and staff is another reason for the poor achievement.

Conclusion

The current trends are quite comforting for customer- but it does pose threats and problems to banks. As we find information technology invading the banking sector, only banks, which used the right technology could come out with success. Banks are required to 'restructure', re-invent and reengineer themselves go meet the necessary performance improvement and get the competitive edge due to the introduction of information technology (e-banking) being an important out pout of; information technology has ushered in an era which is transforming the entire functioning of banks. The tilt in the banks from traditional to modern e-banking services has been welcomed due its advantages, but banks in India are taking time to get rooted; Banks are slow but are going to offer in further more e-banking services to keep in pace with the evolving pattern of customers demand.

The flexibility of e-banking offers unprecedented opportunities for the bank to reach out to its customers. With the rapid expansion of the Internet facilities, e-banking is all set to play a very important role in the 21st century. Banks have to deal with the sophisticated clientele with the help of latest technology like e-banking. Lack of coordination and cyber crimes encroaching. E banking if taken in the right way by banks and customers would take the economy to its best and make it a boon to customers.

Introduction and/or development of information technology will not only affect the banking system of our country but the entire banking system of the world. It is high time to advise and train the banking personnel on the acquisition, installation and use of the information technology. Though there was a cry against the introduction of information technology, it is better to adopt it to face the stiff competition from the ever-dynamic foreign counterpart. As the banks become more sophisticated, the benefits of information technology will grow into leaps and bounds. Further research may be conducted on the feasibility of the introduction of home banking, mobile ATM, office banking, phone banking edger payment system and so on.

Suggestions

In the global era, Banking Industry are increasingly willing to spend more on the customer satisfaction. Though the banking industry is one of the highly regulated industries, it still provides lot of scope for creativity and innovations.

In order to achieve the competitive edge over others standardize the process and bring about quality improvement and get feed back from the customers regarding the quality of services rendered. This will result in customer satisfaction, customer retention, customer acquisition, employee retention and cost reduction.

We have all heard of the digital divide, which is a challenge to be overcome by the banking industry as well. While the average Indian customer may be as technology savvy or even better than his Western counterpart, the cultural aspects of his relationships may necessitate a personal touch to the offerings of banks. Further, all the technology based offering by banks have a bias towards the major towns and cities and the need for reaching the mid size cities as well as the large rural population assumes significance. These pockets hold promises of substantial growth prospects and today with networking capabilities being available at mush higher reliability levels than before and at affordable costs, banks may have to pay attention to these segments of the country as well.

Our society has held a pride of place of being largely knowledge based, ever since the time of the Vedas and the early days of the world. As India develops into a formidable force, it is Information Technology, which holds the key to the process of transformation. Our key strengths lie in knowledge processing and as bankers we have been performing this function quite well both for our customers as well as for the growth of our own organizations. This underlying strength will ensure our key to success. This paper presents and overview on the Banking services in the new millennium.

References

G.S. Mongia, R.K. Sinha, Nationalisation of Banks Retrospect and Prospects.

R.V. Kulkarni, B.L. Desai, Knowledge Based System on Banking Sector.

I.V. Trivedi, Indian Banking in the new Millennium.

M.P. Jaiswal, Anjali Kaushik, e-CRM-Business System Frontiers.

C.S. Rayudu–E-Commerce, E-Business.

E-Commerce-S. Pankaj.

Developing Accounting: Point Publishers, Jaipur 2004, pp. 489-493.

Journal of accounting and finance: Vol. vii, No. 1 Spring, 2004 p. 14-24.

Journal of Accounting and Finance: Vol. ix, No. 1 Spring 2004, p. 76–89.

Banking Finance: Vol vii, No. 7, July 2003, p. 3-4.

Indian Overseas Bank Quarterly News Review: Vol vii No. 1, Jan-March 2004, p. 10-12.

Punjab National Bank Monthly Review: July, 2003, p. 346-353.

The Week: 17 Sep. 2003, p. 28 & 29.

The Banker: Sep. 2004, p. 20.

Information Communication World: Oct. 2004, p. 11-14.

SBI Monthly Review: Oct 2003, p. 521-527.

GLOBALISATION AND RECENT TRENDS IN BANKING

Introduction

The banking sector is in a transitional mode towards a vibrant global market and sophisticated information technology. Due to this changing scenario, banks are paying more attention to expanding their activities from just lending and borrowing to other ends like, insurance merchant banking, leasing, electronic banking etc. Even though these changes were expected after the nationalization of banks in 1969, it was noticed that it had only slow and steady progress necessitating a total revamping of the banking sector. Various reform measures were taken to strengthen the foundation of the system by improving asset quality, enhancing capital and improving profitability along with structural changes in the system. During this transition, banks have seen fierce competition, risk, and revolutionary changes forcing them to take immediate steps to retain market share, redress the grievances of customers as fast as possible by maintaining good ambience, rendering courteous services to customers with the help of latest technological innovations and products.

Globalization and liberalization have forced the banks to think in terms of technology benefits and quality service to customers as future is full of challenges and survival will be a difficult task. The entry of IT infrastructure in the corporate world of banks has brought with it many innovations, in particular the Internet. Though these changes had started with Narasimham Committee's (1992) suggestions for computerization and were followed by Saraf Committee's (1994) recommendations for electronic fund transfers (EFT), Electronic Clearing Services (ECS) and automatic data capture, the banks were actually required to use the BANKET and RBINET and Internet to accommodate itself to the innumerous transactions that had resulted as a result of globalization and liberalization.

The Indian banking industry is not lagging behind, it has started providing services electronically over the internet. These services rendered over electronic media include:

- Phone banking
- ATM–Automatic Teller Machines
- Credit Cards
- Electronic Fund Transfer–EFT
- Shared Payment Network System–SPNS
- Electronic Clearing Service-ECS
- Point of Sale–POS
- D-Mat Accounts
- Electronic Data Interchange
- E-Cheques
- Corporate Banking Terminal

Information Technology

The term "information technology" describes the phenomenon created by the convergence of technologies associated with computing, communication and office systems. In the past, most accounting procedures in banks were paper oriented. With the advent of new techniques like computers, electronic equipments and communication network, the modern accounting system have undergone a sea-change both in their preparation and presentation. The traditional system of preparing the account at quarterly, half yearly and annual lost their relevance since the information are constantly up-dated and made available at any time and anywhere. The information technology enabled the banking organizations to redesign and restructure their functioning.

These services provided by using electronic technology and media are called information technology or electronic banking or e-banking. E-banking has given an opportunity for banks to find solutions to management problems like saving time money and energy or customers by reducing/ minimising paper works, waiting in queues, lack of communication and lack of efficiency. E-banking has provided ease and flexibility in banking operations. The recommendations of Narashimham Committee (1998), for the free and liberal entry of foreign banks in India have further improved the scope for e-banking. As many foreign banks and private sector banks like CITI Bank and ICICI, HDFC banks brought with them IT based products like ATM, credit cards, debit cards, on-line banking etc. This forced the public sector banks and other banks to think on the same lines as these services would help banks to retain their customers, target on banking products and services more effectively to customers.

Customers are also benefited as they are given more free time to indulge in e-commerce business. Therefore, after 1980 throughout the world with majority of banking transactions done through nets or by using information technology. So the information technology solves many problems of the banking industry and very useful to the customers too.

Application of Information Technology

Phone Banking

Bank on phone, provides easy access for customers to have large businesses through telephones. Data are exchanged over the phone regarding any queries, to issue instructions on balance transfer, statement of account, chequebook, stop payments, new schemes, interest rates etc. at any convenient time and place. Telebanking has gone a long way in providing maximum customer satisfaction within the limited infrastructure.

Automatic Teller Machines: (ATM)

Banks in the cities to provide cash dispensation to their customers around the clock install ATMs. Now, the banks provide this facility in a more sophisticated way that a customer of one bank and branch can withdraw from any other banks, at any other branch, nation wide. In developed countries, this service is provided to their blue chip client globally. This is possible only through worldwide networking and communication system.

Credit Cards

These plastic cards enable customers to spend whenever he/she wants within the prescribed limits and pay later. Debit card is a prepaid card with stored value, whereas credit card is post paid with fixed limits. It is seen that spending is higher through debit cards than with credit cards currently CITY Bank and time bank have started with Debit cards and now other banks are also following these to launch their own cards.

Electronic Funds Transfer: (EFT)

Electronic funds transfer is a system of processing and communication of payment through electronic methods. EFT assumes greater significance in the banking system as the RBI also encourages the commercial banks to adopt this technique. Inter and intra bank transfers of funds are now made through this EFT mechanism. Transactions of high value i.e., at least more than one lakh is now made through this cost effective and quick system of settlement. Normally, payments are made through cash, cheques, drafts and credit cards. The latest in this process are the debit card system, charge, digital cash, electronic purse and so on.

SPNS-Shared Payment Network System

SPNS installed by the IBA in the city of Mumbai, enables electronic banking service like cash transactions, extended hours of banking, utility payments, cheques, point of sale facilities by the SPNS can go to any ATM linked to SPNS.

Electronic Clearing Services [ECS]

Electronic clearing of funds from one centre to another for handling bulk transactions like salary, interest, dividend, commission etc., has dispensed the cheques. A part of electronic clearing service is computerized clearing of cheques at metropolitan centers and linking with international communication system of SWIFT. These services have contributed in a great way towards improving the customers services globally. ECS was introduced in India in 1996. It has made it possible for customers to get the funds next day itself.

Point of Sale [POS] Terminal

Payment card at a retail location for electronic transfer of fund is called POS. The client enters his personal identification number [PIN] and confirms the amount due. Customer's account is automatically debited with the amount of purchases and it credits the retailers account POS installed at petrol stations and large retail houses are linked to banks network.

D-Mat Accounts

Transacting shares business through electronic media is called D-Mat. Investor opens an account called Demat

Accounts with DPS. They get shares in electronic form.. Then they send the actual shares to the investor. Investor pays for the opening, maintenance and collection of shares. This has reduced the paper work, bad deliveries; loss of shares and less transaction cost. However delays in demating, higher cost charged by the investors has not given a good start for the growth and scope of Demat in India. Depository participant sometimes make illegal money at the cost of investors. SEBI should find ways to over come this to give a good scope for Demat in India.

Electronic Data Interchange-EDI

EDI refers to the electronic exchange of structure information using telecommunication like payment orders, debits credits, statement of account etc. As part of EDI, satellite communication network is also entering the banks. EDI will very soon do away with branch banking and the customers will identified as ban customer and not branch customer

E-cheques

Digital cheque used by the payer to the payee through internet is called e-cheques. Electronic versions of cheques are issued, received and processed. Most of the banks use e-cheques. A secure means of operation is provided for collecting, payments, and transferring cash flows through this method. The payer issues a digital cheque to the payee and the entire transactions are done through internet

Computerised Accounting

Development in computer has brought about a change in the accounting practices in banks. A wide range of software packages were developed recently, which attributed to the widespread use of computers to increase the information needs. Microcomputer are used to keep records and for processing. Microcomputer is small unit capable of doing calculations, storing data and programmers. These computer range from small personal computer (PCs) to a blue chip "dest top" business computer. The microcomputers are used for word processing, spreadsheet application etc. if the computer is not properly used, and it will result in unfair accounting and loss of information. However, computer provides better information and increases the effiency of the banks.

Data base with different technology such as lost terminal, file server and client server system established all over the world. For creation, manipulation and share information, tools such as Microsoft windows were developed and applied. This Microsoft windows provide graphical user interface, window based word processing along with window based spreadsheet and E-mail package. Information technology now uses geographic information system (GIS) and global positioning system (GPS).

GIS means type in a map to any other type of data. GIS is capable of converting data into pictures and graphs.

GPS means the system, which enabled the precise navigation and targeting of many of the weapons used during the gulf war.

E-Mail

The system of sending messages from one computer to another is known as "E-mail. E-mail originally was introduced in the year 1983 in U.S.A. to send the messages through E-mail, a mini personal computer, one telephone line, a modern and software support is required. Modern is of various types like kotex, robotex, multi-moderna etc. the change for sending a message with 250 characters (bits) through E-mail is Rs2. for express it is Rs. 4. for foreign countries it is Rs.15 per page. If it is sent through telex or fax it costs Rs5 extra for transmission even within our country.

There are different commands like read mail, prepare mail, mail list, status, message forward etc. each of these commands do different functions for example, read mail enables us to read the message sent by other to our computer.

From the above we can understand that E-mail is the most economical and confidential mode of transmission of information globally.

RBI Net: (RBI NET)

This scheme facilitates the transfer of funds by a customer former any bank, any branch, any center to his client at some other center, so other bank and/or branch. Settlements between banks and with the RBI are now a day done through this system. Inter and tntra bank clearing are also done through this electronic communication system.

Internet

Internet is a system interconnected with network worldwide. The increasing popularity of the Internet is the worldwide web (www), which connects millions of servers. In India there are 500 Internet hosts and more than 750 web sites that provide this Internet service. The Internet has 25 million computer buffs and their population explodes at a rate of 10% per month. Internet has found a nest off 150 countries. Arpanet developed by the USA in 1969 was the base for this magical development of Internet. Only those who master the computer commands can work successfully on the Internet.

The Internet has many features. E-mail is one of the simplest facilities available on the Internet. Through this Internet, a subscriber can set up a newsletter, or a discussion through which the participants exchange their views. In the modern age, it is possible to transmit texts; pictures and voices information from anywhere, in any form in the world is accessible to the subscriber at the press of a button and at a very minimum cost.

Computer on the Internet communicate with each other in a number of ways. These methods are called services. The most popular services are:

1. Worldwide web
2. E-mail
3. FTP (file transfer protocol)
4. Use net news
5. ERNET
6. Browser
7. Graphic Viewers
8. New Reader
9. Uniform Resource Locator (URL)
10. Hypertext Transfer Protocol (http)
11. Gopher News
12. Wide Area Information Service (WAIS)
13. Application of information Technology in the Banking System.

The following are the specific Areas where information technology can be used in the banking system.

(i) Preparation and posting in ledger (LAN)
(ii) Portfolio management (genetic algorithm)
(iii) Funds management and transfer (on-line banking)
(iv) Credit appraisal
(v) Foreign exchange transaction
(vi) Opening of letter of credit
(vii) Issue of letter of guarantee
(viii) Decision making at senior manager level
(ix) Employees training and education
(x) Preparation and submission of financial statements

(xi) Identification of fraudulent credit card transactions (neutral network system)

Benefits

The information technology can be administered in the banking system. The application of information technology will help in increasing the operating efficiency of the banking system. Its application will result in saving in cost. The quality of the information can be improved. The branches can provide improved customer services. This will enable the domestic banks to face and challenge the competition from their foreign rivals. There will be a reduction in the staff strength to a considerable extent due to the adoption of information technology. The working condition of the bank branches can be improved.

Benefits of E-Banking Services

- It reduces cost of both in services and administration.
- Overcoming the geographhical barriers.
- Cost minimized for customers.
- It helps to maintain customer loyalty.
- Web site enable banks to develop advertisement.
- Information technology enable banks to deliver products and services.
- Multimedia capabilities offer homogenous branding.
- Online banking encourages promotion of various schemes of the bank.
- Individualised and customized services with the help of integrated customer data.
- Minimising fraud and misappropriation by inter-branch reconciliation.
- Convenience to customers–like card free banking, cash free banking provides a domain of access to banking services.

Reasons for Poor Achievement

1. Poor initial introduction of the information technology concepts in the banks.
2. Improper implementation of techniques of information technology.
3. Improper selection of hardware and software will result in heavy cost and inefficiency.
4. Inadequate suppliers support after the purchase of the IT system.
5. Fear and reluctance among the staff regarding reduction of staff followed by retrenchment due to the introduction of information technology.
6. Brain drain is yet another cause for the poor implementation of the information technology.
7. Lack of co-ordination between the management and staff is another reason for the poor achievement.

Conclusion

The current trends are quite comforting for customer- but it does pose threats and problems to banks. As we find information technology invading the banking sector, only banks, which used the right technology could come out with success. Banks are required to 'restructure', re-invent and reengineer themselves go meet the necessary performance improvement and get the competitive edge due to the introduction of information technology (e-banking) being an important out pout of ;information technology has ushered in an era which is transforming the entire functioning of banks. The tilt in the banks from traditional to modern e-banking services has been welcomed due its advantages, but banks in India are taking time to get rooted. ;Banks are slow but are going to offer in further more e-banking services to keep in pace with the evolving pattern of customers demand.

The flexibility of e-banking offers unprecedented opportunities for the bank to reach out to its customers. With the rapid expansion of the Internet facilities, e-banking is all set to play a very important role in the 21st century. Banks have to deal with the sophisticated clientele with the help of latest technology like e-banking. Lack of coordination and cyber crimes encroaching. E-banking if taken in the right way by banks and customers would take the economy to its best and make it a boon to customers.

Introduction and/or development of information technology will not only affect the banking system of our country but the entire banking system of the world. It is high time to advise and train the banking personnel on the acquisition, installation and use of the information technology. Though there was a cry against the introduction of information technology, it is better to adopt it to face the stiff competition from the ever-dynamic foreign counterpart. As the banks become more sophisticated, the benefits of information technology will grow into leaps and bounds. Further research may be conducted on the feasibility of the introduction of home banking, mobile ATM, office banking, phone banking edger payment system and so on.

References

G.S. Mongia, R.K. Sinha, Nationalisation of Banks Retrospect and Prospects

R.V. Kulkarni, B.L. Desai, Knowledge based System on Banking Sector.

I.V. Trivedi, Indian Banking in the New Millennium.

M.P. Jaiswal, Anjali Kaushik, e-CRM-Business System Frontiers.

C.S. Rayudu–E-Commerce, E-Business.

E-Commerce-S. Pankaj.

Developing Accounting: Point Publishers, Jaipur 2004, p. 489-493.

Journal of Accounting and Finance: Vol. vii, No. 1 Spring 2004 p. 14-24.

Journal of Accounting and Finance: Vol. ix, No .1, Spring 2004, p. 76 –89.

Banking Finance: Vol. vii, No.7, July 2003 p. 3-4.

Indian Overseas Bank Quarterly News Review: Vol vii, No.1, Jan-March 2004, p. 10-12.

Punjab National Bank Monthly Review: July, 2003, p. 346-353.

The Week: 17 Sep. 2003, p. 28 & 29.

The Banker: Sept. 2004, p. 20.

Information Communication World: Oct. 2004, p. 11-14.

SBI Monthly Review: Oct. 2003, p. 521-527.

PART - II
MARKETING

CONSUMERS VIEW ON PETROL PRICES

Introduction

One of the natures gift goes humanity without any return to nature is petrol, which is controlling so many items in our day- to -day life. Many countries thrive on this nature's gift. It has been decided world over that there should be an international control over the petrol prices allowing some margins. Else the petrol producing countries will transact. The control on the price with margin is in innumerable ways. It is now feared this natures gift may get exhausted after few years. So already the alternatives are under exploration.

Petrol is an essential commodity to run the day-to-day life in the world. But India spends more money for petrol to run the transports, factories, purpose of household etc., once it was the family budget but today it is indispensable for the lower people to aristocratic people. In our country utility of the petrol is raising as well as the cost of the petrol is hike.

Present Scenario

Price of the petrol is fixed in our country on the basis of the price of the world market. The producers of petrol adopt the following three components in fixing the price of the petrol.

1. World needs of the petrol
2. Indirect sales of small marketers of petrol.

3. Indirect sellers of petrol by non listed countries.

Indian and China are developing countries in the world since they are consuming more petrol. 40% of the India's expenditure is on diesel. Sales of the transport were hike to 31% in last year in our country. Hence the above-cited information proves the demand of the petrol in our country is rising.

Import of crude oil from other country to India is 70%. India is a fourth place in utilizing and consuming the petrol. In utilizing the petrol America is the first place, China is the second place and Russia is the third place.

America utilizes the one fourth of the world production of the petrol. America produces petrol itself. America utilizes optimum level of petrol for factories, transport and household purposes.

Last year, the cost of the petrol of one barrel was Rs. 1,125/-. Now the cost of the petrol of the one barrel petrol is more than Rs. 3,000/-. India spends nearly 25% on the Import Trade.

The importing expenditure of India, it spends 25% for controlling petroleum products. If not our country raises the price of petrol according to importing price, it will lead to deficit in our budget i.e., 40 crores every year. Our country cannot produce necessary crude oils. Hence we cannot expect the rebate in the cost of petrol.

The Central Govt. maintained Accumulation Maintenance Account for petrol previously. Now, the State Govt maintains it. If the cost of the petrol was raised in other countries in the open market, it was adjusted in Accumulation Maintenance Account earlier. It was not affected the retail seller.

Level of Consumption

Due to continuing rising of the petrol, the Govt. could not adjust in Accumulation Maintenance Account. So it adjusts in its own fund. Honourable Deva Gowda, Former Prime Minister of India closed the above account to solve the problem of our country. Then the Govt. decided to fix the price of the petrol depending upon the rising the petrol cost of other countries. For that open market price for petrol is introduced in 2001. Even if the oil corporation was allowed to raise the cost of the petrol, they have to consult the Central Govt. to raise the price of the petroleum product. The cost of the petrol of 2005 is 25% of the India's budget.

As per survey conducted in 2000 the world consumption of petrol was 7.9 crores barrels per day out of which India's expected consumption was 19 lakes barrels. During 2010 India's expected consumption was 31 lakes and in 2020 it was 41 lakes barrels. In 2030, the demand of the petrol will raise 1.6% per year.

Half of the Price of Petrol is on Tax

Producers of crude oil spend Rs. 450 to 600 per barrels. The cost of the petrol is included to identify the available place of petrol, digging, refine and transportation. Producers of petroleum product sell the petrol in profit of 5 times and VAT is levied on it. Due to excise duty levied on petroleum product, which increases the price of the petrol.

Recently, the cost of the petrol is raised to Rs. 2.50 per litre in our country. Out of Rs. 2.50, the tax is Rs. 1.06 and spend 24 paise for increasing the quality of the petrol. In international market the rising of the crude oil is 70 paise per litre only.

In our country, we are paying tax to the petrol is 57% and diesel 35% and also included road taxes. If our country levies taxes on petrol like other imported commodity, automatically the price hike will be reduced. The Central Govt. levies taxes 10% 0n petroleum product. After refining the petrol the State Govt. Also levies sales tax on it.

In ensuing year, the price of petroleum product may be raised. Indian Oil Corporation expected to raise the cost of the petrol Rs. 8 per litre of petrol.

Obak controls the demand and supply of the petrol, the price of the petrol may hike to $ 75/- dollar in Indian Rs. 3375. It may be raised to $ 100/- dollar of the petrol cost. It can increase the retail seller. The maximum income of the crude oil producers of other countries depends upon crude oil. Like the above factors increase the cost of the petrol. If there is any strike or causes of politicians in Iran & Irack the cost of the petrol may be raised.

China is using the bi-cycle to maintain the utilization of petrol in minimum level. To save the petrol some countries closed the sales for one day.

Suggestions

If India reduces the tax on petrol will reduce the half of the cost of the petrol automatically. Due to providing subsidy to kerosene and gas, the Govt. will not reduce the cost of the petrol.

Either we find out the bio-petrol or using bi-cycle for transporting for short distance will adjust the cost of the petrol and increase the income of our country.

If not we control the consumption of the petrol most of our income will be exhausted on petroleum product.

On our side also there should be self-regulation in limiting use of petrol. There are avoidable occasion where petrol consumption can be minimized e.g., meetings, procession, race, marriages and other such avoidable instances.

Petrol prices are bound to go up as the case of any other commodity. I do not think any other commodity caused remains static.

Reducing the tax on petrol the price hike can control the suggestion by few by reducing the tax on petrol the price hike. By this method, the Govt. should make up this loss in some other sector, which is again coming on the tax- payer. So the permanent solution seems to be reduction in use of petrol wherever it is possible. Reduction of tax extra can be resorted to marginally.

MARKETING OF LEATHER PRODUCTS

Introduction

Leather is an item, which is invariably used in all fields and by all sects of the society. Since it is a natural product available abundantly especially in India, the usage of it is extended in India and across our country. Leather Industry has come to occupy a pre-eminent position in the Indian economy due to its high growth potential for export earnings and employment.

South India particularly Chennai was popular in the global market and nearly 85% of tanned leather had been exported only from this port.

Inspite of the incentives, and concessions offered by the government, use of the sophisticated technology & free import of Machines, Chemicals etc. the leather industries face serious marketing problems.

Some of the marketing problems such as lack of bulk orders, poor image of the product in the world market, insufficient transport facilities, lack of information about the changes in fashion, fluctuations in foreign exchange rates hinder the growth of these units. Effective and timely measures have to be applied to minimise these problems. The research work is to find out the marketing problems and also to know how best the leather industries could improve their exports.

Structure and Organisation

Indian Leather Industry is divided into organized and unorganized sectors. Production in the organized sector is at three levels namely large, medium and small scale. The cottage and the transitional units constitute the unorganized sector. The conversion of raw hides and skins into Semi-Finished leather and the manufacture of leather products for domestic market are done in the unorganized sector.

Organized sector refers to factories that make use of modern technology. There is higher degree of mechanization. Large and medium size units are also known as DGTD units as they have to be registered with the Directorate General of Trade and Development. With command over technology, resources, management, finances and marketing expertise, the organized sector has grown rapidly and in recent years accounted for a major share in the production and exports of finished leather in leather products from India.

The tanning and finishing industry has adopted modern systems but the scale of production in many units is still small. According to the results of the recent Central Leather Research Institute's survey, there were 1,083 tanneries in India with a total installed processing capacity of 62.05 million hides and 161.34 million skins. Of these 75 were reported to be major tanning and finishing units registered with the DGTD.

World Leather Industry at Present

The leather industry in developed countries accounts for half a percent or less of the total manufacturing Industries, while the same is one percent in the developing countries. Among the developed countries France, United Kingdom and Germany are the Principle suppliers of leather.

From the later half of the eighties and nineties, this industry witnessed a decline in many advanced countries due to (1) wage rise (2) reluctance of new entrants (3) high cost operation of leather units in following effluent control laws (4) availability of equivalent leather products at a cheaper rate and (5) Failure of automation to replace the labour intensive operations.

The decline of the leather industry in developed countries like the USA and the U.K would continue to afford an excellent opportunity for the developing countries like India to get a better share of the world market. Besides, the growth of this industry was supported by factors like developed countries dependence on import for a variety of leather goods on India, liberalization of import-export policy, new incentive policy in the promotion of industry and India's own natural strength in raw material resources and skilled but cheap labour force.

In Italy, the tanning units are small units or proprietary concerns with limited facilities. They mainly adopt job work system and each owner specializes in one machine operation. The individual tanner goes to the different machinery job units to get their jobs done. The advantage of this system is that the tanners need not invest in costly machinery and commercial spaces, as these are costly inputs. Hence, considerable economy in the tanneries could be made. The same system prevails in the footwear sector also.

In U.S.A, a corporate approach is mainly followed. There is just 5% to 10% of proprietary concerns in both tanneries and footwear units.

In South America, only Family concerns are prevalent both in the tanning and footwear sectors.

In Germany most leather units are family concerns as that of the Indian small-scale units. In Turkey, manufacture of athletic shoes and garments is carried out mostly by Family concerns.

In India, family concerns are operating at the cottage and small-scale levels. Big industrial houses with partnership have also entered into industry. Recently Public Limited concerns have also been operating. Hence, unlike in other countries, an admixture of all types of concerns is being operated in India.

Perspective of Indian Leather Marketing

Leather, a pliable material from animal hides and skins used for a number of marketable valuable good such as footwear, upholstery, handbags, gloves, musical instrument, belts, saddlery, garments etc., occupies an important position in the industrial scenario of the country. The cattle population is 14% of the world livestock population, which encourages the growth very rapidly during the last decade of its foreign exchange earnings.

Although the tanning in India with an installed capacity of about 116 million pieces of hides and skins with the technical expertise and modern technology, struggles to compete successfully in the domestic as well as global marketing. India, which has sound raw materials base, has been able to occupy the global market with the meager share of only 3.5%. The entry barriers against large scale units, dominants of small scale units in population, leather tanning by cottage sector, non-recovery of hides and skins, inferior quality and damage caused by primitive method of operation in raw material collections, preservation, transportation, curing of hides and skins, quality inadequacy etc., are some of the reckoning features of the Indian Leather Industry which obstruct the competitive edge of the industry.

Leather Industry in Tamil Nadu

Tamil Nadu occupies a pre-eminent position in the leather manufacture and for export it is 70% of the total. The leather sector in Tamil nadu is mostly engaged in tanning and finishing of leather. For instance, as many as 92.3% of the 2175 small-scale units in Tamil Nadu during 2003-04. Were engaged in tanning and finishing of Leather. Although the tanning in India poised for a switch over to production of manufacturing leather article, TamilNadu continues to remain a leading center or tanning in India. More than two-third of processed leather in country is tanned and finished from Tamil Nadu. The tanning and finishing Industry in Tamil Nadu is concentrated in Madras, Ranipet, Dindigul, Ambur, Vaniyambadi, Erode, Perambut and Trichy.

Tamil Nadu occupies a pride place in the industrial leather map of India. Inspite of its pivotal role in growth of Indian leather industry, the export share of leather and leather products has declined drastically during the recent past. For instance, while the export share of Tamil Nadu was 72% in 1989-90 it dropped to 44% in 2003-04.

The decline share of export is attributed to poor diversification of product mix of the industry in the state and mushrooming of leather manufacturing centers in almost all parts of the country and increasing share of contribution to the total export basket of the country.

Location of Leather Industries in Tamil Nadu

In Tamil Nadu the production centers are in the districts of Erode and Vellore. These two together accounted for 75% of the total number of tanneries in the state. These two along with Dindigul and Chengalpattu districts represent practically the entire leather processing capacity, which the state had built up to 1995-96.

The tanneries in the state even attract hides and skins from other states like Uttar Pradesh and Karnataka.

The registered permanent small-scale units in Tamil Nadu by 1989 was 1368 units and it increased to 2175 units during 2004. In all these years maximum concentration of the small scale production units concentrate highly in Vellore, Chennai district occupying the second place and Chengalpattu, Periyar, Salem and Trichy ranking themselves in order.

Leather Industry in Chennai City

Chennai is one of the important pioneer centers of leather industry in India and Tamil Nadu. A number of tanneries in preparation of hides and skins and manufacturing leather products units are located in and around the export market particularly to U.K.

The tanning industry in Chennai has developed significantly during the nineties. Although a few more tanneries were established in Agra, Mumbai and Kanpur, leather goods units and footwear units came to be established elsewhere, the tanning industry came to be concentrated only in Chennai. According to the Directory of SSI units in Chennai District, there are 178 small-scale industrial units engaged in leather tanning and manufacturing of footwear products.

At present, the leather industry in Chennai city undergone virulent structural changes from its earlier production base of curing hides and skins to manufacturing of leather products to the varied requirements of domestic and international markets.

Leather Garment Industry

The turning out of leather from tanning underwent many changes in the history of leather. The leather industry during 21st century witnessed phenomenal growth in leather products industry. There was a radical change from the stage of raw hides and skins to the fabrication of leather garments and their exports.

Leather Garment industry was started a few years ago in India on a small-scale cottage basis. Leather garment making was fairly a labour intensive operation. This sector grew fast due to rise in demand. In India, this sector assumed the role of fabricators only. The leather garments made of sheep leather had good demand in the world market. Damagelessness and strength of sheep leather specially available in Tamil Nadu were the other factors for the promotion of this sector.

Footwear and Components

The manufacture of leather by products in general and footwear and components in particular has turned to be the thrust area of development with high potential of export earnings. However, the share of footwear industry in the world market is hardly 0.9%, but the footwear components received high demand from the shoe manufacturers of U.S.A. and Western Europe who started importing of shoe uppers and other labour intensive parts of shoe-making components.

As far as export of leather shoes are concerned, Italy, South Korea, China, Brazil, Spain, Portugal are the leading countries at the global scenario.

Recently china and a few far countries emerged as centers of low priced leather shoes. The problems like Raw material shortage; technology backwardness, untapped designing skills, managerial deficiency and high cost of production deter the leather footwear Industry leap forward in the international market. Agra and Kanpur are the traditional centers for the manufacture of footwear and components whereas, Chennai and places around Chennai viz, Ambur, Ranipet, and Dindigul and places like Bombay, Calcutta, Delhi emerged as some of important newly established manufacturing centres. Realising the importance of the footwear industry its great potentiality of export earnings, the government of India encourage the growth of the industry by liberalizing the import of the machinery and equipment, raw materials and other consumables required for manufacture of footwear and provision of a number of concessions and incentives particularly to the export promoting units. Moreover, the government has allowed collaboration with the footwear importers and manufacturers abroad mainly to suit the fashion and needs of importing countries. The extension of various facilitating measures encouraged the growth of the industry in a faster pace.

Leather Goods

Unlike the leather garments, the products manufactured by the leather goods Industry have a good domestic market and almost 60%of the production is sold with in the country. Equally Indian leather goods command good market in International Market, despite the fierce competition from China, Korea, Thailand, Hong Kong and Italy.

Finished Leather Goods Industry

This industry is almost from its inception is an export oriented one. Having a surplus of hides and skins owing to a huge cattle population in our country, the production has been mainly for exports. South India was mainly processing and exporting vegetable tanned leather named by the British importers as E.I. tanned hides and skins. In the North Calcutta tanners are processing mostly wet blue chrome hides and skins and the Kanpur tanners making sole leathers from buffalo hides. Tamil Nadu is accounting for bulk of the production of export of E.I tanned hides and skins-almost 90% of the exporters from our country. Somehow, the tanning industry in Tamil Nadu got localized in Vellore District-Particularly in Ambur, Vaniyambadi, Ranipet and Pernambat due to the nearness to the forests.

Leather Industry–Challenges and Opportunities

There is a negative growth in export of leathers in most of the commodities. It indicates not only reversionary situation but also a clear signal to change our marketing strategy in the world market and restructure our industry to meet the changing needs.

The New Exim policy which is going to be in consonance with WTO with its tariff reduction, liberal imports and the emphasis on globalization will certainly have a more positive effect. There is a big gap between the raw material requirement and the raw material availability. The government policy of free import of raw hides and skins, and finished leather is a big boost to the Industry. Import duty reduction on machinery and accessories is a welcome feature. We need a better co-ordination with implementing authorities like, Customs, Banks, DGFT and all those institutions connected with the implementation of EXIM policy.

There is also a need to encourage joint venture in products industry with technology transfer and marketing expertise even without investment from abroad. The causes have to be identified and should offer similar if not the exact facility to attract joint venture, if Indian leather industry wants to be global.

While formulating plan for restructuring Indian leather industry one has to keep in view that industry still needs protection as far as the domestic raw material availability is concerned. W.T.O, which believes in free trade, comprise of members who invariably have strong instinct for self-preservation. They have a double standard where they talk of free trade to exploit other countries raw material. This colonial instinct has got to be distinguished from their real and genuine concern for globalization and free trade. European community complains of restrictive policy in case of Indian leather exports. Advance country like Japan who is a member of W.T.O is protecting its leather industry as it belongs to weaker section of the society. No policy can effectively be implemented if it threatens the self-preservation and survival.

Another area of concern, which will help the healthy growth of the leather industry, is the standardization of domestic raw material. On the face of it, it may look improbable. This exercise is a must if industry has to be viable and healthy. While India a supplier of E.I tanned and wet blue leathers to developed countries. This industry had developed a very scientific method of grading, although it is subjective, but it has helped the importing country. Now whenwe ourselves consume the semi finished leather, the industry is taken for a ride by the unorganized sector. Raw material standardization on scientific basis with all its practical problem will be a task worth doing for the healthy growth of the industry.

The threats, which are likely to act as big deterrent for the development if suitable policy measures are not framed and implemented. The strength of India as a raw material base and cheap labour is challenged by countries like China, East Europe, Latin America etc. Our raw material if not processed according to market needs will have no relevance. China has exploited fully its cheap labour and large reserves of pig leather to cater to the low end of the market with its aggressive marketing techniques.

Indian products be it shoes, bags, garments are out priced in the market. Shoes buyer who used to buy from India, have set up factory in countries like Nepal, Vietnam, Latvia and other. East European countries who enjoy special tariff benefits and buy high quality raw material finished leather from Italy, Spain and make it in these countries and Indian shoes have become less competitive. These emerging markets are posing a threat besides the high profile growth of Chinese leather industry, which is moving up towards market value added production.

Bibliography

Balan, Between you and Leather fashion M/s. Sudha pathipagam, Madras.

Balagopal, T. A.S, Export Management, 2004.

Jane E. Games, Complete Handbook of Leather Crafting, Centeral Leather Research Institute, Madras.

Varshney R.L. (2003), Bhattacharya, B., International Marketing Management, Sultan hand & Sons.

Mosely, G.C. (2001), Leather Goods Manufacture.

Philip, Kotler (2004), Management, Prentice Hall of India Pvt. Ltd., New Delhi.

Rajajee, M.S. (2003), Leather Industry with Special Reference to Exports from South India.

Rajajee, M.S., I.A. Rashed & S.W. Narasimhan (2004), Export Marketing and Management, S.Chand & Company Ltd., New Delhi.

Sankaran, S. (2004), Small Scale Manufacture of footwear, Indian Leather Publication, Madras.

Sarkar, K.T. (2004), Theory and Practice of Leather Manufacture.

Venkatappiah, B. Shoe finishes, CLRI Madras.

Vittal, P.R. (2004), Business Mathematics and Statistics, Margham Publications Madras.

Rajaram, S. (2004), Forex Guide to Traders and Bankers.

PURCHASE DECISION AND CONSUMER BEHAVIOUR

Purchase Decision

In many purchase situations the consumer is confronted with a complex set of alternatives. He has to choose among a variety of products. From a variety of products, he makes selections, based on size, colour, style, models and brands. Also the consumer can make decisions about when and where to buy a certain product, how much he wants to pay and how he will pay for it. Some purchase decisions are routine and may not require much attention. Some other purchase situations involving more cash outlays, safety and health have to be examined. Many product purchases require the evaluation of a variety of economic, social and psychological factors as by the consequences of a wrong decision can be costly.

Consumer Behavior

The term consumer behaviour is defined as the behaviour that consumers display in 'searching for, purchasing, using, evaluating, and disposing of products, services and ideas, which they expect, will satisfy their needs'. The study of behavioral aspects of consumers is the study of how individuals take decisions in spending their available resources–money, time, and efforts–on consumption related items. It includes the study of what they buy, how they buy, when they buy, where they buy, and how often they buy it?

Consumer behavior was a new field of study in the mid to late 1960s. The new discipline borrowed heavily from concepts developed in other scientific disciplines, such as psychology, sociology, social psychology, cultural anthropology and economics.

Decision Process

There are five stages in the buying decision process:

1. Problem recognition (need arousal)
2. Information search (Identification of alternatives),
3. Evaluation of alternatives (evaluation of different brands),
4. Purchase decision (taking a final decision), and
5. Post-Purchase behavior (feed back information i.e., Post-Purchase feelings of satisfaction or dissatisfaction).

The decisions, consumers take in connection with purchases, are influenced by various factors The major factors which influence consumer behaviour are:

1. Culture
2. Sub-culture
3. Social class and
4. Personal factors.

Decision Making Process

Deciding what to buy is one of the consumer's most basic tasks. No buying activity may take place unless this fundamental decision is made. Consumer's product or service decision may encompass not only the generic category of product desired, such as appliances, but more specifically, then narrower range of items, such as kitchen appliances. Consumers must even make decisions on brands, prices, and products features.

The study broadly aims at examining perceptions of the consumers mainly in terms of the information gathered and used for the purpose of the ultimate purchase decision. The pre-purchase behavior of the consumers and and a list of specific factors, which are considered as the evaluation criteria, constitute the basic data for the study. In this process, the goods with reference to which the information relates to are four viz., television, refrigerator, air-cooler and washing machine.

Problem Focus

The present report has hitherto discussed in detail the results of the study on certain aspects of purchase decisions and consumer behaviour with respect to select durable items in the urban areas of Vellore District.

The hot climate, prevailing in Vellore district, induces the middle and upper class people to purchase refrigerator and air-coolers. The employment and high income have motivated the people to purchase television sets and washing machine.

As all the consumers are not alike and their preferences are constantly changing; they prefer differentiated products, which reflect their own special needs, personalities, and lifestyles. People prefer a specific model of durable products among different competing brands for various reasons like handling, comfort, price, appearance, and durability.

Consumers are highly involved in a purchase when it is expensive, bought infrequently and risky. Products involve a decision-making unit, which consists of more than a single person. In a competing market, an analysis of factors that influence purchase decisions is a pre-requisite for the decision–makers of a planned economy because it enables them to have an understanding of the current and future demands of durable products, and match supply with the changing pattern of demand, which will have a great competitive advantage in the market place.

After the World War II, the sellers' market has disappeared and buyers' market has come up. Thus, the marketers of durable products, who understand the relative importance of the information sources used by the consumers, the differences between the users and non-users of the particular sources of information, with reference to selected variables, the evaluation criteria used in making the final decision, and the factors influencing the consumers decision-making process, have a great competitive advantage in the market place. So far, no serious attempts have been made in this field of study in India. The present study of "purchase decision and consumer behaviour of users of durable products" is an attempt in that direction.

Therefore, the approach to study of perceptions and purchase behavior is somewhat complex in orientation. The study concerns itself with two sets of variables; that of information sources, and that which are considered the evaluative criteria. The sources of information are grouped into three broad categories: (a) personal sources. (b) Commercial sources, and (c) retail outlet sources. The evaluative are price (equal and cheaper), model qualities such as appearance, colour and style, brand popularity, availability of services, and spares, product performance, installments payment, availability of the products, ease of operation, reputation and locational attributes of dealers, discounts and warranty. Besides these, some other variables have also been considered as they have impacts on purchase decisions.

Objectives of the Study

The study sets the following objectives for analysis. (i) to examine the relative importance of the information sources used by the consumers in the purchase of four consumer durable products .(ii) to find out the differences between the users and non-users of the particular sources of information in the search process and the dependency of certain selected variables, (iii) to analyze the evaluation criteria used in making the final decision (iv) to identify the factors influencing the consumers in the decision-making process.

Methodology

The approach the following concepts, used in the study, are reviewed.

- Evaluation of consumer information in Economic Thought.
- The Role of information in Marketing.
- The behaviour models.
- Market Information.
- Risk and the Bayesian Approach.
- Nature of Information sources.
- Market Originating Information.
- Consumer Oriented Information.
- Information Search.
- Evaluation Criteria.
- Evaluation Criteria process.
- Decision making process.
- Factors Influencing the Consumer behaviour in Decision making.
- Operational definitions.

The research design, chosen for the present study, includes the choice of the study area, the selection of sample, collection of data and the tools used for analysis.

The Vellore district has been purposively selected for the present study as it has large number of towns, with concentration of large and small-scale industries. Out of the nine municipal towns, four viz. Vellore, Gudiyatam,

Vaniyambadi, and Tirupattur towns were chosen as they have largest number of dealer shops for other selected durable goods.

The consumers of the selected durable goods were traced through the dealers of durable goods in the selected towns. There were thirty dealers, distributed in the four towns, dealing in durable goods-television, refrigerator, air cooler, and washing machine. From the selected dealers, 20 consumers, Who purchased the above said items, was identified. There were 600 consumers of durable goods in the sample frame. Pre-tested questionnaires were served to the selected to the selected consumers. Only 450 filled up questionnaires were returned to the researcher through the dealers.

A structured questionnaire was used to collect the required details from the consumers. The questionnaire was suitably amended after the pre-test through a pilot study. It comprises two sections. Section 'A' was framed to obtain details about the information sources, and section 'B' to collect general information about the consumers of four durable products.

The secondary sources of data on physical features, population, land utilization, agriculture development, industrial development, infrastructure development, health and standard of living were collected from published sources and from the Statistical Department of the Vellore district and the state.

The samples have been used with reference to data gathered in generating factors structures for the products in order to break the variables down to a smaller number of factors that explain the dimensions of consumer perceptions and also decisions.

The same data have been subjected to a further analysis of discrimination so as to bring out the differences between the population with respect to factor, influencing the consumer in making purchase decision and perception variables, sources of information and other related variables that determine consumer behavior in some way. In the two analyses, the study has attempted to gain insights into the consumer behavior of the two groups of consumers (public sector and private sector) as well as classify the respondents into definable groups showing particular characteristics.

The two analyses tested some theoretical suppositions and tried to provide for a classification of variables and consumers, and at the same time, explicitly explaining their behaviors and decisions. Additionally, the study has also looked into information use, the role of media in their perceptions about their durables and how they have helped making decisions for final purchases.

The examination of information sources has been made with a view to find out (a) exposure and (b) effectiveness, in as much as the consumers first hand knowledge of products and brands and further, in using this knowledge gained, in making a purchase decision. In fact, the processes of acquisition through media exposure and the actual purchase have been conceived as two distinct stages of consumer behavior in which the consumers go through a period of evaluation and decision. In as much as these two stages become effective, the relative importance of exposure and effectiveness has been fully evaluated. The evaluation of these two (exposure and effectiveness) was taken to its logical analysis of the dependency between information sources vis-a- vis other selected variables, such as the number of shops/showrooms visited, number of brands considered before the purchase decision was made with respect to the four products. The time lags between contemplation and actual purchase have also been considered to bring out insights on the planning part of a purchase.

Consumer Durable

Selection of Durable Products

The consumerist attitude has been fast catching up in this area. It is evident from the number of durable products possessed by the consumers. Though the middle and upper middle-income group of households possessed a number of durable products, only four durable products have been chosen for the present study because of two reasons: (i) the consumers of these products tend to collect more information about these products, and (ii) the Consumers of these products exercise choice before taking the purchase decision. The durable products chosen for the present study are: Television, Refrigerator, Air-cooler, and Washing machine.

The Indian Consumer

In applying the theories to understand the behavioral dynamics of the Indian consumer, one has to be cautious, most of the buyer behavior models and findings have been developed with the sophisticated western buyer as the focus. But to understand the peculiarities of the Indian consumer, to construct his buying profile, he has to be studied in relation to his environment, his culture and tradition, his educational and economic status, his level of exposure, and the degree of his sophistication. Academic institutions and individual researchers have conducted a few studies on isolated aspects of the buying behavior of the Indian consumer.

Findings

Information Sources

The information sources, which are used by the consumer, are divided into three sections namely (1) Personal Sources (2) Commercial Sources (Including mass media) and (3) Retail Outlet Sources. Personal sources include information from friends, relatives, and neighbors, past experience with the product, personal observation and examination. Commercial source includes advertisement in newspapers, magazines, books, pamphlets, consumer reports, radio, television, roadside hoardings and movie (cinema). Retail outlet source includes information from salesman, personal shop visits and retail outlet. Hence, it is observed that the above three sources of information are mostly used by the consumers in taking decision in the purchase of durable products.

The variable taken as evaluative criteria for purchase decisions are price (equal and cheaper), brand popularity, availability of the product, reputation and location of the dealer, technical performance, service and availability of spare -parts, model qualities [size, colour, style etc.,], warranty, discounts and gifts.

An analysis of evaluation criteria shows that the consumers opt for a good product.

Information Sources and Pre-purchase Behavior

The following inferences are derived from discourse and discussion.

The commercial source has formed as an important item of exposure and effectiveness to the sample consumers.

The consumers utilized the personal sources and retail outlet sources for one to four weeks in decision- making, while the commercial sources they used more than four weeks. While scrutinizing the relationship between time and information sources, the former personal sources found to be independent, and the later commercial and retail outlet sources proved to be a dependent factor.

The consumers have carefully planned before every purchase. So, the level of planning is considered to be a dependent factor related to all other information sources.

Most of the sample consumers have visited one or two shops or showrooms in making purchase decision, but more than two or more shop in case of retail outlet sources. The variables are dependent on each other in the samples.

Inspite of so many information sources, the consumers are drawn towards one or two brands at their final decision, but still brands are proved to be a dependent factor in relation to the three information sources.

Demographic and socio-economic characteristics are deemed to independent variables with few exceptions like age, sex and personal view derived from information sources.

Evaluation Criteria in Purchase Decision

Out of fifteen variables, only first two factors, i.e., Main dimension and bipolar are necessary for the purpose of our epitome and conclusion.

Among the evaluation criteria used in purchase decision the most striking factor is "price", which stands first compared to other variables like installment, discount, prize and gift scheme. Consumers give more importance to economic development or utility in the price of television, refrigerator and air cooler.

With regard to the fourth product, washing machine, price and easy installment are the important criteria used.

The consumers also expressed their preference for goods with discount, easy installment, reputation, operational ease and service charges.

Operational ease also weighed heavily with air cooler product rather than television, refrigerator and washing machine.

Determinant Factors Influencing the Consumer Behavior

In fifteen variables case, the dealer reputation, warranty and special gift are judged to be important factors by the consumers in the purchase of all the four durable products.

In three variables case, the dealers have been rated as good determinant factor in influencing the behavior of the consumers to buy television, refrigerator and air-cooler. But personal source is considered to be a good determinant factor influencing the consumer especially for washing machine.

In four variables case, the brand occupies a good determinant and lead to positive aspect in influencing the consumers to buy more Televisions and refrigerators. Mode of payment also acts as a good determinant factor, influencing the consumer behavior in the purchase of air cooler and washing machine.

Notes and References

1. Michael J. Brennan, (1965), "Theory of Economic Statics", Prentice–Hall, Englewood Cliffs, NJ, p. 4.
2. Richard H. Leftwich, (1966), "The Price System and Resource Allocation", Holt, New York, (3rd ed.,). p. 8.
3. Milton Friedman, (1957), "A Theory of the Consumption Function", Princeton University Press, Princeton, NJ, and J. William Levedhal, June (1980), "The Impact of Permanent and Transitory Income on Household Automobile Expenditures", Journal of Consumer Research, pp. 7.55-66.
4. George Katona, (1963), "The Relationship Between Psychology and Economics", in S. Koch (ed.), Psychology: A Study of A Science. McGraw Hill, New York, p. 603.
5. George Katona, (1980), "Essay on Behavioral Economics", University of Michigan, Ann Arbor, p. 6.
6. Franceso Nicosia, (1966), "Consumer Decision Processes": Marketing and Advertising Implications, Prentice-Hall, Englewood Cliffs, NJ. p. 605.
7. John A. Howard and Jagdish N. Sheth, (1969), "The Theory of Buyer Behaviour", Wiley, New York, p. 607.
8. James F. Engel David T. Kollat and Roger D. Blackwell (1968), "Consumer Behaviour", Holt, Rinechart and Winston, New York, p. 610.
9. James F. Engel David T. Kollat and Roger D. Blackwell (1990), "Consumer Behaviour", The Dryden Press, Chicago, (6th ed.), p. 610.

10. Philip Kolter, (1984), "Marketing Management–Analysis, Planning and Control", Prentice–Hall of India, New Delhi, (5th ed), p. 147.

11. David L. Loudon and Albert J. Della Bitta, (2002), Consumer Behaviour", Concept and Applications, Tata McGraw Hill, New Delhi, (4th ed.) p. 3–51.

PART - III
TAXATION

SERVICE TAX IN INDIA

Introduction

Services in India have been showing a tremendous upswing in growth and has, by and large, outplayed even the manufacturing sector in terms of growth in the past few years. This growth rate in this sector is expected to increase further in the years to come. Consequently, the government considered it fit to levy tax on this sector.

This levy was introduced in 1994 through "Chapter V of the Finance Act, 1994". It must be mentioned that there is no separate legislation covering service tax, which still continues to be governed by the "Chapter V & Chapter VA of the Finance Act, 1994" as amended by the Finance Act, (No.2), 2004. It is pertinent to note that chapter VA of the Finance Act, 1994 has inserted by Finance Act, 2003 to provide for advance ruling law or fact regarding the liability of service Tax.

Service tax is an indirect tax to be borne by the ultimate consumer/customer/client. The service provider cannot claim exemption on the ground that the client has paid the tax and would be obliged to collect the same from the customer, failing which the amount realized from the client would be taken as being inclusive of service tax.

Administration of the Act

The Act is administered by the central Excise Department. A separate cell known as "Service Tax Cell" has been created exclusively to administer Service Tax. The central Board of Excise and Customs (CBEC) has appointed Director General (Service Tax) [DGST] as central Excise officer. The DGST is invested with all powers, in relation to the administration of Service Tax, under the Finance Act, 1994 and Service Tax Rules, 1994, as are exercisable by the Chief Commissioner of Central Excise. It is also provided that certain specified sections of Central Excise Act, 1994 shall apply in relation to Service Tax, as they apply in relation to Excise Duty.

Constitutional Validity

There have been a number of cases challenging the constitutional Validity on the imposition of Service Tax on certain services. However in all these cases, the judgments favoured revenue, notwithstanding certain minor inconsistencies in the constitutional validity of those services, Hence a practical approach would be to focus on the compliance of the law than pondering about the Constitutional validity.

Basic Features of Service Tax

- No basic exemption limit.
- No registration charges. Registration shall be deemed to have been granted, if not granted within 7 days of application.
- Penalty for non-registration or delayed registration.
- Uniform tax rate @ 10% plus Education Cess @ 2% of Service Tax. (prior to 10.09.2004 it was 8% and no such Cess was applicable).
- Certain exemptions are provided in case of services provided to UN, International organizations and SEZ, subject to fulfillment of certain conditions.
- Payment of tax only on realisation of value of taxable service.

- Payment to be on quarterly basis in case of individual, proprietory or partnership firm. Monthly payment in other cases.
- Delay in payment of tax-Simple interest and stringent penalty.
- Credit of tax paid on input service and Duties paid on inputs and capital goods can be availed subject to fulfillment of certain conditions.
- No specific records have been prescribed.
- Half-yearly returns to be filed irrespective of income. Return is in the form of self-assessment.
- Electronic Filing of Returns is now possible for all services.
- Failure to file return may entail penal consequences.
- Central Excise Officers have the power to issue notices for production of documents, accounts etc.
- Central Excise Officers have the power to search premises and seize the documents, books or other things.

Extent of the Act

The Act extends the scope of Service Tax to the whole of India except services provided within the territorial limits of J&K. Services rendered in landmass and territorial waters in designated areas in Continental Shelf and Exclusive Economic Zones are also covered (Notification No.1/2002-ST dt.01.03.2002).

Services Covered

Service tax which initially covered telephone, insurance and share-brokers services have been expanded periodically. The chronological additions services to the service tax net are mentioned in the legislative history of services. The number of services that are chargeable to tax as on September 2004 is

71. The Services of Goods Transport Agency would be taxable from a date to be notified.

Revenue

The revenue from service tax, which was Rs.407 Crores in year 1994-95, has been rising consistently and rose to around Rs.5,000 Crores in the year 2002-03 and to around Rs. 7.890 crores in the year 2003-04. The target revenue for 2004-05 is around Rs. 20,000 Crores. However majority of revenue still arises from the 5 core services viz telephone, insurance, share-brokers, advertising agency and courier agency.

Legislative History of Services

Finance Act, 1994 introduced service tax with the following 3 services namely:

1. Telephone;
2. Insurance (other than life insurance); and
3. Stock Broker.

Subsequently in 1996, the said levy was extended to 3 more services namely:

1. Advertising Agency;
2. Pager; and
3. Courier Agency.

The Major Expansion was Started in 1997 when the following 12 services were included:

1. Consulting Engineer;
2. Custom House Agent;
3. Steamer Agent;
4. Clearing & Forwarding Agent;
5. Manpower Recruitment Agency;
6. Air Travel Agent;
7. Goods Transport Operator;

8. Outdoor Catering;
9. Pandal or Shamiana Contractor;
10. Mandap Keepers
11. Tour Operator (exempt till 31-3-2000); and
12. Rent-cab (exempt till 31-3-2000).

In 1998, the services of goods transport operators, outdoor catering and pandal/shamiana contractor were removed from the taxable services while 12 more services were added as detailed below;

1. Architect;
2. Interior Decorator;
3. Management Consultant;
4. Chartered Accountant;
5. Cost Accountant;
6. Company Secretary;
7. Security Agency;
8. Real Estate Agent & Consultant;
9. Market Research Agency;
10. Credit Research Agency;
11. Under-writer; and
12. Slaughter Houses (discontinued from 28.2.2000).

Finance Act, 2001 has expanded the services to cover the following 15 services:

1. Scientific or Technical Consultancy;
2. Photography Studio or Agency;
3. Convention;
4. Telex;
5. Telegraph;
6. Facsimile;

7. On-line information and Database Access and/or Retrieval Services;
8. Video-tape production;
9. Sound recording;
10. Broadcasting Agency;
11. Services auxiliary to insurance (including broking and agency services;
12. Banking & other Financial Services 9excluding insurance);
13. Post Services;
14. Authorized Service Station Service or repair of vehicles, incl. Two wheelers; and
15. Leased Circuit.

Finance Act, 2002 has expanded the services to cover the following 10 services:

1. Beauty parlour;
2. Cable operator;
3. Cargo Handling Service;
4. Dry Cleaner;
5. Event Manager;
6. Fashion Designer;
7. Health & Fitness Centre;
8. Life Insurance Business (Taxable from 10-9-2004);
9. Rail Travel Agent's Service; and
10. Storage & Warehousing Service.

Finance Act, 2003 has expanded the services to cover the following 8 services:

1. Business Auxiliary Services;
2. Commercial Training or Coaching Centres;
3. Commissioning and Installation Agency;

4. Franchisor;
5. Internet Café;
6. Maintenance or Repair Services;
7. Technical Testing and Analysis Agency; and
8. Technical Inspection and Certification Agency.

Finance Act, 2004 has expanded the services to cover the following 13 services:

1. Aircraft Operator;
2. Airports Authority;
3. Construction Service;
4. Forward Contract Service;
5. Goods Transport Agency (to be notified later);
6. Holder of Intellectual Property Rights;
7. Opinion Poll Agency;
8. Organiser of Business Exhibition;
9. Outdoor Caterer;
10. Pandal or Shamiana Contractor;
11. Programme Producer;
12. Survey and Exploration of Minerals; and
13. Travel Agent.

VALUE ADDED TAX IN INDIA

TAX THAT'S NOT TAXING -There is no such thing as a good tax

—Winston Churchill

Introduction

Vatman says.. Whether you like it or not you have to deal with value added tax (VAT). Different from sales tax, VAT will change how business is done in India. Here is how it will affect trader, industrialists, exporters and consumers and why it is good for India.

"When my baby grows up, s/he will become a collector!". Many mothers made this wish while cuddling their babies over 50 years ago in India. Now their wishes have come true. With the introduction of VAT from 1 April 2005, every VAT–payer becomes a government tax collector! As its name implies, you pay tax to the government every time you add value to any goods by first paying this tax to your suppliers, and then collecting it from your customers. So you become an unpaid tax collector by paying VAT to the government every month or three months.

This is no jock, for VAT is the most important and the most wide ranging tax reform in India in the last half a century. It is to be introduced on 1 April 2005 because the new financial year starts on this date in India. Thus it is a practical date for starting this new tax that means almost a new system of doing business and keeping its accounts.

VAT is the most far reaching tax reform in India because it replaces the sales tax, the dreaded Sales Tax inspections, your unpleasant trips to sales tax offices and filling up of many forms. You calculate the amount of VAT you have to pay by self-assessment.

Moreover, you will not pay many other taxes that you have been paying for so long. VAT will bring a major change in the way you do business because you will have to issue cash memos or other documents for everything you sell. So the system of 'cash business' will almost be over in a few years.

VAT Not New

VAT is not new. For many, many years in country, traders and industrialists have been paying an excise duty. An excise duty is nothing more than a central VAT on production. When goods are produced and cleared from the factory gate, they are liable to an excise duty. When A produces goods and sells it to B, A charges an excise duty, and B pays the excise duty. When B uses those goods in the production of other excisable goods and he sells to C, B charges excise duty, but takes credit for the excise duty that he has already paid and then C pays the excise duty. So VAT is not new. It is an old tax applicable all over India. What is new is that after the decision of the central government, and all state governments, VAT replaces Sales Tax in the states.

How is VAT Different From Sales Tax?

There is a major difference between sales tax and VAT. While in sales tax, the ultimate consumer pays tax on some part(s) of the product more than once, in VAT, the consumer pays tax on the value of the entire product only once. Let us take an example of a car on which we pay a sales tax. The car manufacturer does not make all the parts that go in to it. The manufacturer makes the body shell and fixes many different auto parts in to it-the engine, a gearbox, the radiator, the steering wheel, the tyres , the battery and all other parts. He makes some, buys some, and imports others. Most inputs are Sales Tax paid. Suppose some one makes the steering wheel or the tyres and sells them to the carmaker, the Sales Tax is paid on these parts. When the car is made, it uses the parts on which the sales tax is has already been paid, and when you buy this car, you pay the Sales Tax on the value of whole car. This means that if there is a part like the engine, which was valued at Rs. 50,000 and the car is valued at Rs3 lakh, you again pay sales tax on Rs. 50,000 because that has already gone into the cost of the car. Thus you pay tax more than once. If you look into the making of engine, then you will realize that the engine manufacturer paid Sales Tax on the steel that was used to make the engine. Sometimes you end up paying more than one tax as well. Thus you are paying more taxes under Sales Tax. But not under VAT.

Under VAT, everyone who buys a product pays this tax. After adding value to it, he sells it to his buyer. The seller adds VAT and collects it from the buyer. After a period of time, the trader fills up the VAT return, deducts the VAT he has paid to his supplier, and pays the difference (or the tax on the value he has added) to the government. This goes down the entire chain until it reaches the final customer or consumer who pays tax only once all along the line. This VAT reduces the tax paid by the consumer.

Why Traders Fear VAT

In spite of the benefits why are traders so unhappy with VAT? Traders have been strongly protesting against the introduction of VAT and have delayed its introduction a number of times. The answer is simple. Many traders do not usually give cash memos or bills when they sell goods to their customers. If the customer asks for a cash memo or a bill, he/she is told, "you will have to pay Sales Tax". Many customers do not want to pay more, so they say they can do without the bill and they tell the shopkeepers, "I don't want a bill, so don't charge me sales tax." So less sales tax is collected and paid to the government. And traders are carrying on what is known as 'cash business'. This means that the true income is never known and no Income Tax is paid on a lager part of the income. VAT will not only increase the amount formerly collected as Sales Tax but also Income Tax. " The whole purpose of VAT is to tackle tax evasion," said Dr Asim Kumar Dasgupta, the chairman of the state level VAT Empowerment Committee of the State Finance Ministers in a new paper interview. "Is it fair for traders or anyone else to keep on evading taxes?" he asked.

Traders are unhappy with VAT because

- All traders must issue cash memos/cash bills/invoices, etc., under the law. So ' cash business' will be very much reduced if not finished altogether in a short time. They will have to pay more VAT and, later on, more income tax.
- Trader/businessmen will have to learn and introduce new and different accounting systems for the new VAT procedures. Traders will have to do much more paperwork.
- Opening stocktaking is a problem. Traders need to show the tax-paid stock they have on 1 April 2005. This means a special stocktaking exercise.
- Tax-paid opening stocks may be much lower than actual stocks,
- No input tax credit or VAT refund is available on inter-state purchases.
- Buying from companies currently under a tax exemption scheme will attract VAT.

- Traders think that refunds or input tax credit may be difficult to obtain from the VAT department.
- New registration for VAT may take time and create problems.
- Traders claim that VAT will increase prices and thus lower demand for their products.
- It is a new and different tax from sales tax and everybody dislikes change.

VAT is User-friendly

These fears are unfounded because:

- Those, hard to get and harder to fill, Sales Tax forms will be a thing of the past. Once the basics are learnt, VAT will simplify tax calculation and filling of VAT returns. With tax payable only on the value added, calculating the tax amount will become easier. Just calculate the difference on your purchases and sales during the period of the return you want to file, and you get to know your tax payable or how much you can claim as refund. Pay your tax according to this calculation or claim your refund. This is self-assessment how you assess your tax by yourself. As simple as this.
- Small dealers with a turnover of less than Rs5lakh a year do not pay any VAT. So they cannot complain. The next group of dealers with a turnover of between five and 50lakh have two choices: just pay one per cent of the turnover as VAT and there is no need to keep detailed VAT account book, or register for VAT, if you find it useful for your business.
- You are automatically registered for VAT if you are paying Sales Tax. Your sales tax number becomes your VAT number. New registrations are supposed to take less time than Sales Tax registration.

- Under VAT registration, there is no need to get official permission to add more goods to your registration certificate (RC) as was the case with Sales Tax.
- Uniform tax rate all over India on 550 most traded products.
- Uniform rate of tax (VAT) at 12.5 per cent, 4 per cent, and 1 per cent all over the country.
- Opening stocks on 1 April 2005 can get the refund of sales tax paid on them as long as purchases are made within one year before this date, i.e., after 31 March 2004. Any tax paid on unsold stock will be taken as input tax credit and can be adjusted at the time of payment of your VAT in the next return.
- VAT credit will be uniformly allowed for tax paid on purchases within the states from the VAT payable by a dealer. Credit will be calculated on a uniform basis all over India. This will cover raw materials, capital goods and items purchased for resale by VAT payers.
- Self-assessment by the traders.
- VAT is relatively simply to administer. Taxpayers do not have to make frequent trips to the Sales Tax Office. The entire system of Sales Tax is outdated and has been replaced by VAT in 130 countries.
- No Tax Inspectors 'harassment. You can file an objection against any VAT order passed by any authority. If no decision has been taken on your objection within a fixed period, then it is deemed to be in your favor. Fair, isn't it?
- Less number of taxes as VAT will abolish many other taxes.
- No VAT is payable on exports. Exporters will get tax refunds on their purchases and other inputs.

Why Industrialists Fear VAT

- New accounting system. Computer accounting packages do not contain VAT modules and so require be replacing or updating.
- Complicated accounting when buying or selling goods from or to other states.
- No credit allowed for taxes paid on purchases made outside a particular state. This means Central Sales Tax or local tax charged by other states cannot be claimed.
- Production costs will have to be recalculated as the tax structure on raw material may change.
- Distribution costs may be hit with stockists and wholesalers having to pay VAT. Sales to stockists and distributors will attract VAT. Some manufacturers may have to absorb some increases in their maximum retail price (MRP).
- Branch transfers likely to lose part of Input Tax Credit.
- No credit for Central Sales Tax or taxes paid in other states.
- Buying from companies currently under a tax exemption scheme will attract VAT.
- Stock transfers to branches may at first create VAT accounting problems.
- More appeals and court cases will be filed to clarify many points of VAT laws. This means additional time and expense.
- The market share of some industrialists may decrease may decrease as their comparative advantages decline due to VAT.

The Industrialists Need Not Worry Because

- Once they have learnt how the VAT system works, they pay a single tax instead of many taxes.

- VAT also means paying fewer taxes than before.
- Once VAT comes in to operation, there will be more demand for their goods since the prices will come down.
- VAT is designed to make India into one market or a common market without tax barriers. Under the Sales Tax system, a Declaration From is required for inter-state transport of goods and this is collected at the border check-post.
- Multiple taxes add 25-30 per cent to the prices of Indian goods in world markets. With VAT, these prices will come down. So Indian exports will become more competitive in world markets and industrialists can export more of their goods to the 135 countries under the World Trade Organization that has common trade policies.
- VAT will ensure more efficient production and lower prices of goods. Sales Tax interferes with the choice of inputs and outputs due to different tax rates on them. Since VAT means uniform taxes, it gives them a choice based on other considerations than the taxes on an input or output.
- Under VAT the system of Input Tax Credit will promote production efficiency of investments. Investment decisions will not, therefore be based on differences in tax in different states or on some states giving tax holidays.
- VAT credit is available on purchase of raw materials in a state against the sale made within that state or another state from the home state.
- Industrialists will continue to enjoy the Sales Tax incentives earlier granted by a state.
- VAT paid on the purchase of capital goods con be claimed over 36 months

- No VAT is payable on exports. Exporters will get the tax refund on their purchases and other inputs.

Why Exporters Fear VAT

- VAT will have to be paid on all local purchases and although it can be claimed later on, it could have a negative effect on cashflows. Exporters may opt for monthly VAT returns to get refunds more quickly.
- Pricing of their goods may be affected with VAT in some cases.

The exporters will enjoy some advantages under VAT, including;

- Can get Input Tax Credit or VAT refund for purchases of capital goods over 36 months.
- Costs could be lower in the long run.
- Move towards Cenvat instead of Modvat.
- With zero-rating on exports, the rate of tax on export goods will be zero and yet credit will be given on VAT paid on inputs. Exporters will get input tax credit within three months. This will make exports more competitive.

Why Customers Fear VAT

- Customers or consumers fear that prices of all goods will go up after VAT. Many goods including some farm produce will be taxed at a higher rate of 12.5 per cent and other goods such as salt will be taxed.
- A trader or businessman will charge more and blame it on VAT. True, this has happened in some countries when VAT was first introduced.

In fact, a short time after VAT is introduced, prices decline as the customers get to know how it works. This is the experience of many countries and is expected to be the same in India. Most states in India tax personal products such as soaps, shampoos, shaving creams, toothpastes etc., at 16 per cent. Under VAT, this product will be taxed at 12.5 per cent and so their prices will decline. Moreover, VAT means that they do not pay cascading taxes or tax on tax amounting to higher taxes as they did under the Sales Tax system.

What are the Problems in Introducing VAT?

- Traders and industrialists have to learn new VAT accounting systems and introduce them from 1 April 2005. Thus they need a great amount, if not full, information on how to work with VAT. They have to spend more time in learning VAT laws and procedures.
- Lack of adequate and widespread information on VAT procedures: state governments need to spend much more than they have planned, to inform everyone about VAT in all languages and through all media. Since they are going to collect more tax amounting to thousands of crores, they should spend much more so that the introduction of VAT faces fewer problems.
- The VAT departments and officers need to be better prepared in knowing the new system. VAT forms should be easily available and user-friendly. The department must have a major change in their mindset-from regulators to facilitators-in their dealings with the taxpayers.
- All states should have uniform VAT documents to help in quick and easy accounting by companies operating in more than one state and for VAT claims.
- Removal of non-tax barriers-goods permits and transport documents introduced by local governments and states.
- Phasing out of Central Sales Tax (CST). It is planned to phase it out in two years.

- VAT must cover services as it does in most other countries. Once you can claim VAT on the goods you buy you should also be able to claim VAT on the services you get. For example, you get VAT on raw materials but you pay Service Tax on repairs to your machinery that you cannot claim.
- Not all state taxes are included in VAT but this should be done.

Is VAT Good For India?

Yes, VAT will help India to grow faster and stronger because:

- India will become a single common market with no state checkpoints for entry of goods and not market of 28 different states and seven union territories. When goods can be transported all over India without paying additional state and local taxes, their prices will come down. Thus the demand by domestic consumers will go up. So industrialists will produce more and expand their factories and create more jobs.
- Indian goods become cheaper in world markets as they bear less taxes and so Indian exports will increase. This means more industrial expansion and more income.
- With simple and transparent tax laws and administration, there will be no 'Inspector Raj'.
- Wherever VAT has been introduced, the tax collected by the government rises many times. Haryana was the first state to introduce VAT in 2003 and its revenue increased by 27.5 per cent in two years. More revenue means more facilities and services for the citizens. This means more roads, bridges, hospitals, schools and other facilities for the citizens.
- All this results in higher economic growth. It is estimated that the Indian economy will grow by up to 2 per cent

more per year when VAT is in full use. This means that India will move faster on the road to becoming an economic superpower in the world.

Speaking at an ASSOCHAM seminar on VAT in December 2004, the Finance Minister of India, Mr. P.Chidambaram, said that the government will speak and explain and exhort people to come into the new tax system. The VAT empowered committee of all state finance ministers is a national level monitoring body. All state finance ministers have agreed that they will not make any change in the VAT law without the express consent of the Empowered Committee. So, the Empowered Committee has become a self-regulating body of all finance ministers of all states and will meet every month to regulate VAT.

"In the last 50 years, VAT has been a very, very important tax measure. It is a very important tax reform. We cannot afford to either stumble or fall, and with your cooperation, with your support, with the support of the Chambers, I am confident that we will not stumble. We will not falter. We will not fail. We will make a success of VAT," said MrChidambarm.

Vatman says

Industrialists and exporters have welcomed VAT. Consumers will learn to live with it. But traders know it will greatly reduce if not end, 'number two business'. So they will be paying more as VAT than as Sales Tax, and, a few years later , much more income tax. VAT is a tax whose time has come and you cannot do business without it. So read on and learn more about it...

PART - IV
INSURANCE

LIFE INSURANCE IN THE GLOBAL ERA

Introduction

The Life Insurance Industry plays a vital role in the economic development of our nation. It mobilizes long -term savings for investment and for retirement. Life Insurance acts as one of the attractive financial instrument that assures security with attractive returns. India stands Fifth in Asia in terms of Insurance premium collection. Currently, out of more than one billion people in India, only seventy million are covered by Insurance.

What Is Life Insurance?

Life Insurance is a contract for payment of a sum of money to the person assured (or failing him/her, to the person entitled to receive the same) on the happening of the event insured against. Usually the contract provides for the payment of an amount on the date of maturity or at specified dates at periodic intervals or on unfortunate death, if it occurs earlier.

Need For Life Insurance

Life is full of uncertainties. Life Insurance is concerned with two hazards that stand across the life path of every person viz.

- Dying prematurely, leaving a dependent family to fend for itself.
- Living too old without visible means of support.

To safeguard the policy–holders against these risks, the Insurance companies collect premium. It settles the claims on the maturity period or on the death of the insured, whichever is earlier.

Life Insurance provides the following benefits:

- Life Insurance guarantee financial protection against risk of death of the policy–holders.
- It encourages thrift. Long term saving is made painless due to the availability of installment facilities.
- Loans can be raised on the sole security of a policy, which has acquired a paid–up value.
- Life Insurance policy is accepted as security for the commercial Loan/Housing Loan.
- Tax relief in Income Tax is available for amounts paid by way of premium subject to the Income Tax rules in force.
- A suitable Insurance plan can be taken to meet specific needs that are likely to arise in future, such as children's education, marriage provision e.t.c.

Life Insurance in India

The Life Insurance business in India had its origin in 1818 with the establishment of the Oriental Life Insurance Company in Kolkata. The Indian Life Assurance Companies Act, 1912 was the First measure to regulate Life Insurance business. Later in 1928 the Indian Insurance Companies act was enacted, which was amended in 1938 with the sole objective of protecting the interest of the insuring public.

Life Insurance Corporation of India was formed in September 1956 by passing L.I.C. Act, 1956 in Indian Parliament, with the capital contribution of Rs. 5 crores from the Government of India. The funds generated by it are invested in the avenues that benefit the society. It acted as a monopoly insurer and catered the life cover risk of the public.

In the wake of reform processes and passing of Insurance Regulatory and Development Authority (IRDA) Bill through Indian Parliament in 1999, Indian Insurance was opened for Private Companies. Liberalisation and Globalisation have allowed the entry of foreign players in the Life Insurance sector.

Life Insurance Industry had ten and two entrants in the Year 2000-2001 and 2001-2002 respectively. One additional entrant was made on 6th February 2004. At present there are fourteen companies in Life Insurance Sector. The Funds earlier generated by L.I.C. have been diversified with other new insurers. We should wait and see how the new players are going to boost up our economy.

List of Private Life Insurers

Sl. No.	*Date of Reg.*	*Name of the Company*
1.	23.10.2000	HDFC Standard Life Insurance Company Ltd.,
2.	15.11.2000	Max Newyork Life Insurance Co.Ltd.
3.	24.11.2000	ICICI Prudential Life Insurance Company Ltd.,
4.	10.01.2001	Kotak Mahindra Old Mutual Life Insurance Ltd.,
5.	31.01.2001	Birla Sun Life Insurance Company Ltd.,
6.	12.02.2001	Tata AIG Life Insurance Company Ltd.,
7.	30.03.2001	SBI Life Insurance Company Limited
8.	02.08.2001	ING VYSYA Life Insurance Company Private Limited
9.	03.08.2001	Bajaj Allianz Life Insurance Company Limited
10.	06.08.2001	Metlife India Life Insurance Company Pvt. Ltd.,
11.	03.01.2002	AMP Sanmar Life Insurance Company Limited
12.	14.05.2002	Aviva Life Insurance Company Limited
13.	06.02.2004	Sahara India Life Insurance Company Ltd.,

Source: www.irdaindia.org.

Present Scenario

The Primary reason for buying an Life Insurance Policy is to protect us from vagaries of life. People invest in Insurance not for returns; rather for regrettable necessities. Previously, people buy Insurance for tax concession. Now, the actual goal of the investors while buying the Insurance is retirement planning, protecting family against contingencies, asset creation and children higher education.

In India Insurance is sold and not bought. The agents/ Advisors by using various strategy sell the product by convening the customers. More over, they Push Policies with the highest premium to pocket a higher commission. With the entry of private and foreign players in the Life Insurance business, people have got a host of options to choose from. Radical changes are taking place in customer profile due to the changing life style and social perception, resulting in erosion of brand loyalty. Higher customer aspirations lead to new expectations and compel him to move towards the insurer who provides him the best services in time. To survive, the focus of the modern insurers is shifted from mass marketing paradigm to a customer-centric relationship.

Market Share (In %)

Years	*L.I.C.*	*Private players*
2001 – 2002	98.00	2.00
2002 – 2003	94.34	5.66
2003 – 2004	87.00	13.00
2004 – 2005	82.00	18.00

Source: Insurance Chronicle , February 2005 Insurance Watch July 2005

The private players have increased their market share from two per cent in 2001-2002 to eighteen per cent in 2004-2005. Among them ICICI prudential is ranked first in capturing the market followed by Bajaj allianz and Brila sun life.

The joint ventures in the private sector are progressing satisfactorily but few of them are not running well. It has come to the fore that AMP Sanmar is about to sell their interest to other players. Moreover, private players have planned to increase their market share to thirty per cent in the next five years. L.I.C. has to enrich its strategy to with held its share.

Modern Selling Approach

The consultative approach to selling is the 21st century approach that helps customers and prospects to buy. A consultant makes calls and sales just like any other sales person. The difference is in their attitude, their approach and their commitment. Here, the customer is seen as a person to be served and not a person to be sold. It helps the purchaser to make an intelligent decision. The four-step process includes:

- Need discovery
- Selection of the product
- Need satisfaction presentation, and
- Serving the sale

This approach to selling requires understanding of concepts and principles borrowed from the fields of psychology, communications, and sociology and needs a lot of personal commitments and self–discipline from the seller.

The commitments referred are:

1. Finding and understanding the needs of the customers.
2. Partnering with the customers.
3. Helping the customers to achieve his business and other objectives by the purchase of the product or service.
4. Believing that your products/services are a great fit with your customer's needs, and
5. Believing in yourself and your ability to help the customers in solving their problems.

A consultant is willing to forego short-term gains to achieve greater long–term benefit to him and the customers he serves. He builds relationships on a foundation of trust, respect and performance. Moreover, consultants don't sell– they're specialists who make recommendations to help the prospect to buy. They act as a professional and offer real-world solutions that make sense to the customer.

Conclusion

The Indian Insurance market is becoming more aggressive day-by-day. The opening of the Insurance sector paved the way to generate phenomenal growth in the Insurance business and innovation and introduction of new products. It has become complex situation for the buyers of Insurance product due to variety of products and multiplicity of choices before the customer. Moreover, one should make sure that the product he is buying shall meet his specific needs and affordable both in terms of cost and return. This study focuses on the marketing strategy to be adopted by the modern insurer to retain the existing customers and to attract new ones in this global era.

References

'Insurance principles and practice' (2004) M.N. Mishra, S. Chand and Company Ltd., New Delhi.

'Introduction to Insurance' (2005) Marks S. Dorfman, Prentice hall, Inc, Engle Wood Cliffs, N.J. 07632.

Principles of Risk Management (2003) George E.Rejda, Pearson Education (Singapore Pvt. Ltd.), New Delhi.

Insurance–Fundamental, Environment and Procedures (2004) B.S. Bobla, M.C. Garg, K.P. Singh, New Delhi.

Principles and Practice of Insurance (2005) Dr. P. Periasamy, Himalaya Publishing House, Mumbai.

Journals

Southern Economist, March 1, 2004.

Insurance Watch, August, 2004.

Insurance Watch, September, 2004.

Insurance Watch, December 2004.

Insurance Chronicle, February, 2005.

Insurance Watch, July, 2005.

Websites

www.irdaindia.org

www.bimaolnline.com

www.lic.india.com

www.eastindiavyapaar.com.

LIFE INSURANCE IN RURAL INDIA

Introduction

Agriculture is the base of Indian economy. About 75 per cent of the population depends on agriculture and its allied activities for their livelihood. Rural India generates income over $ 200 billion per year. Life Insurance sector acts a corner stone of our country. Healthy rural development leads to economic stability. Currently, out of more than one billion people in India, only seventy million are covered by Insurance.

What is Life Insurance?

Life Insurance is a contract for payment of a sum of money to the person assured (or failing him/her, to the person entitled to receive the same) on the happening of the event insured against. Usually the contract provides for the payment of an amount on the date of maturity or at specified dates at periodic intervals or on unfortunate death, if it occurs earlier.

Need for Life Insurance

Life is full of uncertainties. Life Insurance is concerned with two hazards that stand across the life path of every person viz.

- Dying prematurely, leaving a dependent family to fend for itself.
- Living too old without visible means of support.

To safeguard the policy–holders against these risks, the Insurance companies collect premium. It settles the claims on the maturity period or on the death of the insured, whichever is earlier.

Life Insurance provides the following benefits:

- Life Insurance guarantee financial protection against risk of death of the policy–holders.
- It encourages thrift. Long term saving is made painless due to the availability of installment facilities.
- Loans can be raised on the sole security of a policy which has acquired a paid–up value.
- Life Insurance policy is accepted as security for the commercial Loan/Housing Loan.
- Tax relief in Income Tax is available for amounts paid by way of premium subject to the Income Tax rules in force.
- A suitable Insurance plan can be taken to meet specific needs that are likely to arise in future, such as children's education, marriage provision etc.

Life Insurance in India

The Life Insurance business in India had its orgin in 1818 with the establishment of the Oriental Life Insurance Company in Kolkata. The Indian Life Assurance Companies Act, 1912 was the First measure to regulate Life Insurance business. Later in 1928 the Indian Insurance Companies act was enacted, which was amended in 1938 with the sole objective of protecting the interest of the insuring public.

Life Insurance Corporation of India was formed in September, 1956 by passing L.I.C. Act, 1956 in Indian Parliament, with the capital contribution of Rs. 5 crores from the Government of India. The funds generated by it are invested in the avenues that benefit the society. It acted as a monopoly insurer and catered the life cover risk of the public.

In the wake of reform processes and passing of Insurance Regulatory and Development Authority (IRDA) Bill through Indian Parliament in 1999, Indian Insurance was opened for Private Companies. Liberalisation and Globalisation have allowed the entry of foreign players in the Life Insurance sector.

Life Insurance Industry had Ten and Two entrants in the Year 2000-2001 and 2001-2002 respectively. One additional entrant was made on 6th February 2004. At present there are fourteen companies in Life Insurance Sector. The Funds earlier generated by L.I.C. have been diversified with other new insurers. We should wait and see how the new players are going to boost up our economy.

Current Scenario

The Primary reason for buying an Life Insurance Policy is to protect us from vagaries of life. With the entry of private and foreign players in the Life Insurance business, people have got a host of options to choose from. Radical changes are taking place in customer profile due to the changing life style and social perception, resulting in erosion of brand loyalty. Higher customer aspirations lead to new expectations and compel him to move towards the insurer who provides him the best services in time. To survive, the focus of the modern insurers is shifted from mass marketing paradigm to a customer-centric relationship.

Market Share (IN %)

Years	*L.I.C.*	*Private players*
2001–2002	98.00	2.00
2002–2003	94.34	5.66
2003–2004	87.00	13.00
2004–2005	82.00	18.00

Source: Insurance Chronicle , February 2005 Insurance Watch July 2005.

The private players have increased their market share from two per cent in 2001–2002 to eighteen per cent in 2004

–2005. Among them ICICI prudential is ranked first in capturing the market followed by Bajaj allianz and Brila sun life. Moreover, private players have planned to increase their market share to thirty per cent in the next five years. L.I.C. has to enrich its strategy to with held its share.

Life insurance sector has an excellent potential from the rural market. The mass in rural have understood that Life Insurance is not only a place for Investment but also a source for securing their lives and there by ensuring their dependents livelihood. This paved the way for Indian Life insurers to focus their attention on rural people to market their products. Moreover, IRDA has set stiff rural target for Life Insurance companies.

Modern Selling Approach

In India Insurance is sold and not bought. The agents/ Advisors by using various strategy sell the product by convening the customers. Moreover, they Push Policies with the highest premium to pocket a higher commission. The consultative approach to selling is the modern approach that helps customers and prospects to buy. A consultant makes calls and sales just like any other sales person. The difference is in their attitude, their approach and their commitment. Here, the customer is seen as a person to be served and not a person to be sold. It helps the purchaser to make an intelligent decision. The four-step process includes:

- Need discovery
- Selection of the product
- Need satisfaction presentation, and
- Serving the sale

This approach to selling requires understanding of concepts and principles borrowed from the fields of psychology, communications, and sociology and needs a lot of personal commitments and self–discipline from the seller.

The commitments referred are:

1. Finding and understanding the needs of the customers.
2. Partnering with the customers.
3. Helping the customers to achieve his business and other objectives by the purchase of the product or service.
4. Believing that your products/services are a great fit with your customer's needs, and
5. Believing in yourself and your ability to help the customers in solving their problems.

A consultant is willing to forego short-term gains to achieve greater long–term benefit to him and the customers he serves. He builds relationships on a foundation of trust, respect and performance. Moreover, consultants don't sell– they're specialists who make recommendations to help the prospect to buy. They act as a professional and offer real-world solutions that make sense to the customer.

Globlisation has made the industry to be aware that the rural customers need a different packaging on the product front. Insurer has to design the products as to satisfy their emerging needs. Moreover, proper awareness must be created among the rural customers about their new and innovative products.

Conclusion

The Indian Insurance market is becoming more aggressive day-by-day. The opening of the Insurance sector paved the way to generate phenomenal growth in the Insurance business and innovation and introduction of new products. It has become complex situation for the buyers of Insurance product due to variety of products and multiplicity of choices before the customer. Moreover, one should make sure that the product he is buying shall meet his specific needs and affordable both in terms of cost and return. This study focuses on the marketing strategy to be adopted by the modern insurer to retain the existing customers and to attract new ones from rural market.

Bibliography

Books

'Insurance Principles and Practice' (2004), M.N. Mishra, S. Chand and Company Ltd., New Delhi.

'Introduction to Insurance' (2005) Marks S. Dorfman, Prentice hall, Inc, Engle Wood Cliffs, N. J. 07632.

Principles of Risk Management (2003) George E. Rejda, Pearson Education (Singapore Pvt. Ltd.) , New Delhi.

Insurance–Fundamental, Environment and Procedures (2004) B.S. Bobla, M.C. Garg, K.P. Singh, New Delhi.

Principles and Practice of Insurance (2005) Dr. P. Periasamy, Himalaya Publishing House, Mumbai.

Journals

Southern Economist, March 1, 2004.

Insurance Watch, August, 2004.

Insurance Watch, September, 2004.

Insurance Watch, December 2004.

Insurance Chronicle, February, 2005.

Insurance Watch, July, 2005.

Websites

www.irdaindia.org

www.bimaolnline.com

www.lic.india.com

www.eastindiavyapaar.com.

IMPACT OF LPG ON THE LIFE INSURANCE SECTOR

Introduction

Life Insurance sector is an important cornerstone to our economy. It plays an important role in mitigating life uncertainties. Life insurance acts as one of the attractive financial instrument that assures security with attractive returns. India stands Fifth in Asia in terms of Insurance premium collection. Currently, out of more than one billion people in India, only seventy million are covered by Insurance. The sector is governed by Insurance Act, 1938, the Life Insurance Corporation Act,1956, Insurance Regulatory and Development Authority (IRDA) Act, 1999 and other related Acts.

Need for Life Insurance

Life is full of uncertainties. Life insurance is concerned with two hazards that stand across the life path of every person viz.

- Dying prematurely, leaving a dependent family to fend for itself.
- Living too old without visible means of support.

To safeguard the policy-holder's against these risks, the Insurance companies collect premium. It settles the claims on the maturity period or on the death of the insured, which ever is earlier.

Life Insurance provides the following benefits:

- Safeguards oneself and family for future requirements
- Encourage savings
- Tax rebate
- Protection from the claim made by creditors
- Security against personal loan, housing loan etc.,

History of Life Insurance in India

The business of life Insurance in India in its existing form started in India in the year 1818 with the establishment of the Oriental Life Insurance Company in Calcutta.

The milestones in the Life Insurance business in India are:

1912 : The Indian Assurance Companies Act enacted as the first statue to regulate the Life Insurance business.

1928 : The Indian Companies Act enacted to enable the government to collect statistical information about Life Insurance.

1938 : Earlier legislation consolidated and amended to by the Insurance Act with the object of protecting the interest of the insuring public.

1956 : 245 Indian and Foreign Insurers and provident societies taken over by the central government and nationalised. LIC formed by an Act of Parliament viz. LIC Act,1956 with a capital contribution of Rs. 5 crore from the Government of India.

The funds generated by LIC are invested in the avenues that benefit the society. It acted as a monopoly insurer and catered the life cover risk of the public till the enactment of Insurance Regulatory and Development Authority (IRDA) Act, 1999.

Impact of LPG

Global integration of financial markets resulted from de-regulating measures, technological, information explosion and financial innovations. With the entry of private and foreign players in the Life Insurance business, people have got a host of options to choose from. Radical changes are taking place in customer profile due to the changing life style and social perception, resulting in erosion of brand loyalty. Higher customer aspirations lead to new expectations and compel him to move towards the insurer who provides him the best services in time. To survive, the focus of the modern insurers shifted to a customer-centric relationship. WTO deserves that the customers must receive different insurance packages that would benefit him as well as the society in time. Moreover, it supports the globalisation, which enables the customer to choose independenly among the various packages offered by the global players. Thereby, it secures the interest of the customers.

In the wake of reform processes and passing of Insurance Regulatory and Development Authority (IRDA) Bill through Indian Parliament in 1999, Indian Insurance was opened for Private Companies. Liberalisation and Globalisation have allowed the entry of foreign players in the Life Insurance sector.

Liberalisation and Privatisation

India's economic development made it as a most lucrative Insurance market in the world. Before the year 1999, there was monopoly state run LIC. In the wake of reform process and passing Insurance Regulatory and Development Authority (IRDA) Act through Indian parliament in 1999, Indian Insurance was opened for private companies.

Liberalization on the Insurance sectors has allowed the foreign players to enter the market with their Indian partners. Most of the foreign Insurers have joined within the local market. India offers immense possibilities to foreign Insurers since it is the world's most populous country having over a billion people.

Life Insurance industry had ten and two entrants in the year 2000-2001 and 2001-2002 respectively. One additional entrant was made on 6th February 2004. At present there are fourteen companies in Life Insurance Sector. The Funds earlier generated by LIC have been diversified with other new insurers. We should wait and see how the new players are going to boost up our economy.

Competition

Private and Foreign entrants in the Life Insurance Industry made others difficult to retain their market. Higher customer aspirations lead to new expectations and compel him to move towards the insurer who provides him the best service in time. It becomes less viable for them even to maintain the functional networks or competitive standards and services. To survive in the Industry they analyses, the emerging requirements of the policyholders and are in the forefront in providing essential services and introducing novel products. Thereby they become niche specialist, who provides the right service to the right person in right time.

Market Share (IN %)

Years	*L.I.C.*	*Private players*
2001–2002	98.00	2.00
2002–2003	94.34	5.66
2003–2004	87.00	13.00
2004–2005	82.00	18.00

Source: Insurance Chronicle , February 2005 Insurance Watch July 2005.

The private players have increased their market share from two per cent in 2001–2002 to eighteen per cent in 2004–2005. Among them ICICI prudential is ranked first in capturing the market followed by Bajaj allianz and Brila sun life.

The healthy competition in the sector enabled the giant insurer of our mother country–LIC to reduce its market share to eighty two per cent in 2004-2005. More over, private life insurers have planned to capture thirty per cent of the market share in the next five years. LIC has to enrich its approach to with held its share.

Information Technology

Insurers are the earlier adopters of technology. Because of the Information revolution, customers are free to choose from a wide range of new and innovative products. The Life Insurance companies are utilizing the Information technology applications for better customer service, cost reduction, new product design and development and many more.

New technology gives the policyholders better, wider and faster access to products and services. The impact of Information Technology in Insurance business is being felt at an accelerating pace. In the initial years IT was used more to execute back office functions like maintenance of accounts, reconciling broker accounts, client processing etc. With the advent of "database concepts", these functions are better integrated in an administrative efficiency.

The real evolution is however emerged out of Internet boom. The Internet has provided a brand new distribution channels to the Insurers. The technology has enabled the Insurer to innovate new products, provide better customer service and deeper and wider insurance coverage to them. At present, Insurance companies are giving customers a distinct claim id to track claims on-line, entertaining on-line enrollment, eligibility review, financial reporting, billing and electronic fund transfer to its benefit clan customers.

Product Innovations

Life Insurance is all about making sure your family has adequate financial resources to make those plans and dreams come true. It provides financial protection to help your family or business to manage after your death.

Few of the Life Insurance policies are:

- Whole life policies
- Endowment policies
- Money-back policies
- Annuities/Children's policies
- Pension schemes

Companies will need to constantly innovate in terms of product development to meet ever changing consumer needs. Understanding the customer better will enable Insurance companies to design appropriate products, determine price correctly and increase profitability. Since a single policy cannot meet all the Insurance objectives, one should have a portfolio of policies covering all the needs. At present, most of the Life Insurers are concentrating on the pension schemes and thereby enriching their market share. Moreover, with increased commoditization of insurance products, brand building is going to play a vital role.

Distribution Network

While companies have been successful in product innovation, most of them are still grapping with right mix of Distribution Channels for capturing maximum market share to build brand equity, building strong and effective customer relationships and cost effective customer service.

While the traditional channel of tied up advisors or agents would be the chief distribution channel, insurer should innovate and find new methods of delivering the products to customers. Corporate agency, brokerage, Bancassurance, e-insurance, cooperative societies and panchayats are some of the channels which can be tapped by the insurers to reach the appropriate market segments. Now-a-days, the urban masses are tapped with the new techniques provided by Information Technology through Internet. Moreover, the rural masses are attracted by the consultative approach adopted by the Life Insurance agents/advisors.

Customer Education and Services

Life Insurance, is never bought but sold. The key industry drivers are related to life style issues in terms of perceiving insurance as a savings instrument rather than for risk cover, need based selling, quality of service and customers awareness.

In the present competitive scenario, a key differentiator is the professional customer service in terms of quality of advice on product choice along with policy servicing. Servicing focus on enhancing the customer's experience and maximizing his convenience. This calls the effective CRM system, which eventually creates sustainable competitive advantage and enables to build long lasting relationship.

Marketing Life Insurance in the New Millennium

In India Insurance is sold and not bought. The agents/ Advisors by using various strategy sell the product by convening the customers. More over, they Push Policies with the highest premium to pocket a higher commission. The consultative approach to selling is the 21st century approach, that helps customers and prospects to buy. A consultant makes calls and sales just like any other sales person. The difference is in their attitude, their approach and their commitment. Here, the customer is seen as a person to be served and not a person to be sold. It helps the purchaser to make an intelligent decision. The four-step process includes:

- Need discovery
- Selection of the product

- Need satisfaction presentation, and
- Serving the sale

This approach to selling requires understanding of concepts and principles borrowed from the fields of psychology, communications, and sociology and needs a lot of personal commitments and self–discipline from the seller.

The commitments referred are:

1. Finding and understanding the needs of the customers.
2. Partnering with the customers.
3. Helping the customers to achieve his business and other objectives by the purchase of the product or service.
4. Believing that your products/services are a great fit with your customer's needs, and
5. Believing in yourself and your ability to help the customers in solving their problems.

A consultant is willing to forego short-term gains to achieve greater long–term benefit to him and the customers he serves. He builds relationships on a foundation of trust, respect and performance. Moreover, consultants don't sell–they're specialists who make recommendations to help the prospect to buy. They act as a professional and offer real–world solutions that make sense to the customer.

Conclusion

In the global era, Life insurance companies are increasingly willing to spend more on the customer satisfaction and brand building exercises. Though the industry is one of the highly regulated industries, it still provides lot of scope for creativity and innovations. As our industry is predominantly dominated by personal selling and personalized services many a time the service standards vary based on the intermediary involved in the process. In order to achieve the competitive edge over others standardize the process and bring about quality improvement and get feed back from the customers regarding the quality of services rendered. This will result in customer satisfaction, customer retention, customer acquisition, employee retention and cost reduction. This paper presents an overview on the Life Insurance Sector in the new millennium.

References

Books

Insurance Principles and Practice-M.N. Mishra, S. Chand and Company Ltd., New Delhi.

Introduction to Insurance-Marks S. Dorfman, Prentice hall, Inc, Engle Wood.

Cliffs, N.J. 07632.

Journals

Southern Economist, March 1, 2004.

Insurance Watch, August, 2004.

Insurance Watch, September, 2004.

Insurance Chronicle, February, 2005.

Insurance Watch, July, 2005.

Websites

www.irdaindia.org

www.bimaonline.com

www.licindia.com

www. asiantradehub.com

INDIAN INSURANCE: MODERN MARKETING APPROACH

Introduction

The Insurance sector plays a vital role in the economic development of our nation. It acts as a mobiliser of savings, financial intermediary, promoter of investment activities, stabiliser of financial markets and a risk manager. India is still an under-insured country in the world. It is at the 18th position among Life Insurance markets and 28th in Non-Life Insurance markets in the world. This indicates that there is a huge potential, yet to be explored.

History of Insurance in India

The business of life insurance in India in its existing form started in India in the year 1818 with the establishment of the Oriental Life Insurance Company in Kolkatta.

Some of the important milestones in the Life Insurance Business in India are:

1912 : The Indian Assurance Companies Act enacted as the first statue to regulate the Life Insurance business.

1928 : The Indian Companies Act enacted to enable the government to collect statistical information about Life Insurance.

1938 : Earlier legislation consolidated and amended to by the Insurance Act with the object of protecting the interest of the insuring public.

1956 : 245 Indian and Foreign Insurers and provident societies taken over by the central government and nationalised. LIC formed by an Act of Parliament viz. LIC Act, 1956 with a capital contribution of Rs.5 crore from the Government of India.

The General Insurance Business in India, on the other hand, can trace its roots to the Triton Insurance Company Ltd., the first General Insurance Company established in the year 1850 in Kolkatta by the British.

Some of the important milestones in the General Insurance Business in India are:

1907 : The Indian Mercantile Insurance Ltd., set up, the first company to transact all classes of general insurance business.

1957 : General Insurance Council, a wing of the Insurance Association of India, frames a code of conduct for ensuring fair conduct and sound business practices.

1968 : The Insurance Act amended to regulate investments and set minimum solvency margins and the Tariff Advisory Committee set up.

1972 : The General Insurance Business (Nationlisation) Act, 1972 nationlaised the general insurance business in India with effect from 1st January 1973. 107 insurers amalgamated and grouped into four companies viz. the National Insurance Company Ltd., the New India Assurance Company Ltd., the Oriental Insurance Company Ltd., and the United India Insurance Company Ltd. GIC incorporated as a company.

The funds generated by LIC and Public Sector General insurers are invested in the avenues that benefit the society. They solely acted as public undertaking insurers and catered the life cover and general risk cover of the public till the enactment of Insurance Regulatory and Development Authority (IRDA) Act,1999.

Current Scenario

Global integration of financial markets resulted from de-regulating measures, technological information explosion and financial innovations. Liberalisation and Globalisation have allowed the entry of foreign players in the Insurance sector. With the entry of private and foreign players in the Insurance business, people have got a lot of options to choose from. Radical changes are taking place in customer profile due to the changing life style and social perception, resulting in erosion of brand loyalty. To survive, the focus of the modern insurers shifted to a customer-centric relationship.

Liberalisation and Privatisation

India's economic development made it a most lucrative Insurance market in the world. Before the year 1999, there was monopoly state run LIC transacting life business and the General Insurance Corporation of India with its four Subsidiaries transacting the rest. In the wake of reform process and passing Insurance Regulatory and Development Authority (IRDA) Act through Indian parliament in 1999, Indian Insurance was opened for private companies.

Liberalisation on the Insurance sectors has allowed the foreign players to enter the market with their Indian partners. Most of the foreign Insurers have joined within the local market. India offers immense possibilities to foreign Insurers since it is the world's most populous country having over a billion people.

Insurance industry had ten and six entrants in life and non-life sector respectively in the year 2000-2001. The industry again saw two and three entrants in the life and non-life business respectively in the year 2001-2002. One additional entrant was made both in the life and in non-life business in 2004 and 2005 respectively. At present there are fourteen companies each in Life and General Insurance. The Funds earlier generated by the state owned insurers have been diversified with other new insurers. We should wait and see how the new players are going to boost up our economy.

Competition

Private and Foreign entrants in the Insurance Industry made others difficult to retain their market. Higher customer aspirations lead to new expectations and compel him to move towards the insurer who provides him the best service in time. It becomes less viable for them even to maintain the functional networks or competitive standards and services. To survive in the Industry they analyse, the emerging requirements of the policyholders/insureds and they are in the forefront in providing essential services and introducing novel products. Thereby they become niche specialists, who provide the right service to the right person in right time.

In August 2005, the private players in the life insurance business have increased their market share to 23.93 per cent. Among them ICICI prudential is ranked first in capturing the market followed by Bajaj Allianz and HDFC Standard. In the General Insurance sector the private players have captured 26.10 per cent. Among them ICICI-Lombard is ranked first, followed by Bajaj Allianz and IFFCO-Tokio.

The healthy competition in the sector enabled the State owned insurers of our mother country to reduce its market share to 76.07 per cent and 73.90 percent in life and non-life business respectively. Moreover, private insurers have planned to increase their market share in the next five years. The public insurers have to enrich its approach to withheld its share.

Information Technology

Insurers are the earlier adopters of technology. Because of the Information revolution, customers are free to choose from a wide range of new and innovative products. The Insurance companies are utilizing the Information technology applications for better customer service, cost reduction, new product design and development and many more.

Market Share (%) - August 2005

Life Insurers		*Non – Life Insurers*	
1. LIC	76.07	1. New India	21.41
2. ICICI Prudential	6.91	2. National	17.11
3. Bajaj Allianz	4.75	3. United India	17.11
4. HDFC Standard	2.98	4. Oriental	17.02
5. Brila Sunlife	1.72	5. ICICI- Lombard	8.04
6. Tata AIG	1.66	6. Bajaj Allianz	6.15
7. SBI Life	1.46	7. IFFCO-Tokio	4.00
8. Max New York	1.28	8. Tata-AIG	2.89
9. Aviva	1.08	9. ECGC	2.50
10. Kotak Mahindra Old Mutual	0.71	10. Royal Sundaram	2.17
11. ING Vysya	0.54	11. Cholamandalam	1.22
12. AMP Sanmar	0.46	12. HDFC-Chubb	0.89
13. Met Life	0.37	13. Reliance General	0.75
14. Sahara Life	0.03	14. Agriculture Insurance Co.	—
Private Total	23.93	Private Total	26.10
Public Total	76.07	Public Total	73.90
Grand Total	100.00	Grand Total	100.00

Source: www.irdaindia.org.

New technology gives the policyholders/insureds better, wider and faster access to products and services. The impact of Information Technology in Insurance business is being felt at an accelerating pace. In the initial years IT was used more to execute back office functions like maintenance of accounts, reconciling broker accounts, client processing etc. With the advent of "database concepts", these functions are better integrated in an administrative efficiency.

The real evolution is however emerged out of Internet boom. The Internet has provided brand new distribution channels to the Insurers. The technology has enabled the Insurer to innovate new products, provide better customer service and deeper and wider insurance coverage to them. At present, Insurance companies are giving customers a distinct claim id to track claims on-line, entertaining on-line enrollment, eligibility review, financial reporting, billing and electronic fund transfer to its benefit clan customers.

Product Innovations

Insurers are continuously innovating new products based on forward looking models. They have developed new products addressing the new challenges in society and products to address the hazards from new environmental issues. Companies will need to constantly innovate in terms of product development to meet ever changing consumer needs. Understanding the customer better will enable Insurance companies to design appropriate products, determine price correctly and to increase profitability. Since a single policy cannot meet all the Insurance objectives, one should have a portfolio of policies covering all the needs.

Product development is made possible by integrating actuarial, rating, claims and illustration systems. At present, the Life Insurers are concentrating on the pension schemes and the Non-Life Insurers on many innovative schemes of various realms and thereby enriching their market share. Moreover, with increased commoditization of insurance products, brand building is going to play a vital role.

Distribution Network

While companies have been successful in product innovation, most of them are still grapping with right mix of Distribution Channels for capturing maximum market share to build brand equity, building strong and effective customer relationships and cost effective customer service.

While the traditional channel of tied up advisors or agents would be the chief distribution channel, insurer should innovate and find new methods of delivering the products to customers. Corporate agency, brokerage, Bancassurance, e-insurance, cooperative societies and panchayats are some of the channels which can be tapped by the insurers to reach the appropriate market segments. Now-a-days, the urban masses are tapped with the new techniques provided by Information Technology through Internet. Rural masses are attracted by the consultative approach adopted by the Insurers. Moreover, they attract the customers through telephone and mobile also.

Customer Education and Services

Insurance is a unique service industry. The key industry drivers are related to life style issues in terms of perceiving insurance as a savings instrument rather than for risk cover, need based selling, quality of service and customers awareness.

In the present competitive scenario, a key differentiator is the professional customer service in terms of quality of advice on product choice along with policy servicing. Servicing focus on enhancing the customer's experience and maximizing his convenience. This calls the effective CRM system, which eventually creates sustainable competitive advantage and enables to build long lasting relationship.

Modern Marketing Approach

Marketing strategies for insurance in the emerging scenario could be understood in terms of the following steps:

$$R \longrightarrow STP \longrightarrow MM \longrightarrow I \longrightarrow C$$

Here, R	=	Market Research
STP	=	Segmentation, targeting, positioning
MM	=	Marketing Mix

I = Implementation

C = Control

Having done market research and finalising on segmentation, targeting and positioning the strategy would focus on the marketing mix namely, Product, Price, Place and Promotion. While determining the implementation methodology, the four characteristics viz. Intangibility, Inseparability, Perishability and Variability gives rise to certain unique requirements that deserve careful attention while formulating the marketing strategy for insurance. After implementation, the insurers should concentrate on the effective control that would enhance their business.

In India Insurance is sold and not bought. The agents/ Advisors by using various strategies sell the product by convencing the customers. Moreover, they push Policies with the highest premium to pocket a higher commission. The consultative approach to selling is the modern approach, which helps customers and prospects to buy. A consultant makes calls and sells just like any other sales person. The difference is in their attitude, their approach and their commitment. Here, the customer is seen as a person to be served and not a person to be sold. It helps the purchaser to make an intelligent decision. The four-step process includes:

- Need discovery
- Selection of the product
- Need satisfaction presentation, and
- Serving the sale

This approach to selling their products requires understanding of concepts and principles borrowed from the fields of psychology, communications, and sociology and needs a lot of personal commitments and self–discipline from the seller.

The commitments referred are:

- Finding and understanding the needs of the customers.
- Partnering with the customers.
- Helping the customers to achieve his business and other objectives by the purchase of the product or service.
- Believing that your products/services are a great fit with your customer's needs, and
- Believing in yourself and your ability to help the customers in solving their problems.

A consultant is willing to forego short-term gains to achieve greater long–term benefit to him and to the customers he serves. He builds relationships on a foundation of trust, respect and performance. Moreover, consultants don't sell–they're specialists who make recommendations to help the prospect to buy. They act as a professional and offer real–world solutions that make sense to the customer. Today, the insurers adopt this technique and thereby go on increasing their market share.

Conclusion

In the global era, Insurance companies are increasingly willing to spend more on the customer satisfaction and brand building exercises. Though it is one of the highly regulated industries, it still provides lot of scope for creativity and innovations. As our industry is predominantly dominated by personal selling and personalized services many a time the service standards vary based on the intermediary involved in the process. In order to achieve the competitive edge over others standardize the process and bring about quality improvement and get feed back from the customers regarding the quality of services rendered. This will result in customer satisfaction, customer retention, customer acquisition, employee retention and cost reduction. This paper focuses on the marketing approach adopted by the modern insurers to withheld their existing customers and attract new ones.

References

Books

Insurance Principles and Practice-M.N. Mishra, S. Chand and Company Ltd., New Delhi.

Introduction to Insurance-Marks S. Dorfman, Prentice hall, Inc, Engle Wood Cliffs, N.J. 07632.

Indian Insurance Industry-D.C. Srivastava and Shashank Srivastava, New Century Publications, Delhi.

Journals

Southern Economist, March 1, 2004.

Insurance Watch, August, 2004.

Insurance Watch, September, 2004.

Insurance Chronicle, February, 2005.

Insurance Watch, March, 2005.

Insurance Watch, July, 2005.

Indian Journal of Marketing, July, 2005.

Life Insurance Today, September, 2005.

Websites

www.irdaindia.org

www.bimaonline.com

www.licindia.com

www. asiantradehub.com

PART - V
AGRICULTURE

GROW MORE TREES

Introduction

The most essential requirements of human are wood and "wood products". It is not possible to live without using them during a human's lifetime. For house hold windows, doors, table, chair, pencil, slate, etc. For agriculture, plough, carts, wheels, green manure leaf, shades, cattle feed, fence, oil, fruits, cotton and small timber, wood and wood products are needed.

The carbondioxide, which we breathe out, gets purified by the trees and returns to as oxygen. A tree in its lifetime gives 17 lakh worth benefit to humanity. From cradle to grave-yard, wood and "wood products" form part and parcel of human life.

Necessity of Growing More Trees

If we visualise two hillocks one with tree growth and other without i.e., barren. After rains there is flood from the barren hills because the entire downpour goes off as floods. Whereas the other one much of the rainfall gets soaked in and this water comes out in trickles and the rivers arising out of these hillocks as supply water perennial to the ponds, pools, lakes such as streams, rivulets and all water sources. The water table is very much high in these sources. This is the basis for agriculture. So the "world forest policy" says for the welfare of all departments each country should have one third (33%)

of its land area under forest. This is our national forest policy also. But our nation as a whole has only 22% land area as forests and in Tamil Nadu it is only 17%. So in both in center and state the minimum requirement is not there. To make up this only both govt's are implementing social forests, avenue forest, creating forest in lakes and ponds and along railways, along roads, agro-forestry and waste land development programme.

Our forefathers who had robust-knowledge were maintaing "illuppai topes", Tamarind topes, and sacred groves etc.

Trees are required for paper, rayon, artificial silk, rail coaches, railway sleepers, ships, boats, gun, aircraft etc. So tree planting is essential. But it should be made economical too.

For houses within the premises, we can grow drumstick, guava, lime, curry leaf plants. We should adopt policy like "one tree for one family". Forest department selling is around 20 varieties plants at concessional rates (for fruits, shades, fence, green leaf manure, oil seeds, folder, fuel, small timber etc). people should avail of this. Trees can be planted in the village grazing ground, village common grounds, educational institution, factories, private land holdings, and agricultural fields.

Suggessions

In educational institutions at the admission time, students must be required to plant a sapling and nourish it till he leaves the institutions. Some marks may be allotted for this tree culture. If this is done meticulously there may not be enough space after a few years to plant any more plants in that institution. The object is achieved.

On behalf of forest and agricultural departments, nurseries to be raised with in the institutions, for enriching the students also.

Green belt to be created along roads, railways, water channels, canals, airport, factories etc. Tree cutting to be prohibited and in unavoidable cases ensure two trees are planted. Green car scheme i.e. When a car is purchased the quantum of smoke it may be giving out in its life time to be estimated and to off-set an amount should be collected from the buyer and amount spent for growing more trees.

To counter population explosion and increase in number of factories (though these are necessary evils) tree panting is essential

To safeguard nature, it is in our hand. So reduce population, plant more trees, make surrounding green, live a long-life.

Following plants are suitable and so suggested for the following soils and climate.

Sandy Soils

Sisso, Pungan, Acacia, Casuarinas, Vitex, Thespesia, Anacadium, Teco mella

Saline Soils

Acacia,Butea,Tamarix, Neem, Eucalyptus, Prosopis.

Swampy Soils

Eugenia, Largerstroemia, Salix, Butea, Eucalyptus.

Stiff Clay End Soils

Acacia, Terminalia, Butea, Neem, Tamarind Acbizzia, Frost hardy, Dalbergia, Morus, Zizyphus, Bamboo, Eugenia, Hardwickia, Bischofia, Prosopis,Vitex, Pinus Vitex.

Drought Area

Acacia, Ficus, Hard wickia, Prosopis, Lagerstroemia, Eugenia, Pungan, Lannea, Diospyros, Anogissus, Anacardium, Zizyphus, Salvadora, Capparis, Neem.

Canal Banks

Teak, Sisso, Eugenia, Acacia, Mangi fera, Ailan thus, Terminalia, Pungan, Neem, Tamarind, Madhuca, Eucalypetus.

Road Side Avenues

Eugenia, Tamarix, Dalbergia, Samania, Ficus, Pungan, Spathodia, Peltaphorum, Delonix, Vateria, Madhuca, Cedrela, Bauhinia, Polyalthia, Ailanthus, Jacranda Neem, Cassia.

NO LOSS IN AGRICULTURE

—A Case Study

It is commonly spoken that our age old agriculture which is the backbone of our economy is no more profitable and worthwhile. But I am not inclined to go with this. I sustain my views by many instances. I cite a case study in support of my belief.

Says 'Indian forests service' retired high official Chief Conservator of forests Mr.V.Jayaraman, I.F.S., in an exclusive interview with him, the following are elicited. He retired during 1993. The above official is doing agriculture instead of choosing retired life in "TAMASA"; money lending; chits ,finance etc., avenues. He had chosen agriculture which is mostly spoken as in loss; but to the above bureaucrate it is not so .How he explains.

Water Conservation, Management and Harvesting

He has 20 acres of agricultural lands at Mudalai Maduvu, Ponneri, Jolarpettai, Tirupatur Taluk, Vellore District. This compact area is encircled with stone pillars and barbed wire. This entire land has been partitioned in to 90 bits. There are two open wells, each having two bore wells. All the 90 bits are connected by PVC Pipes. The result is there is no loss of time in water reaching the destination; No loss of land enroute; No loss of see page and evapo transportation. No cleaning of water passage. There is out let in each bit. These are the few points of water management.

Coconut

Out of 400 trees, 350 are yielding and are given on bienneal lease. Besides, planting of good varieties of coconut seedlings are planted every year. Coconut leaves are woven and sold, used for thatching. Broom are made out. These trees draw nourishment from the agricultural chops where they stand. Above are the sailent aspects.

Crop Varieties

Any part of the year not less than 10 types of crops are cultivated. Even during drought, no field is empty. Depending on the availability of water drought resistant crops, are resorted to. For instance, cumbu (penni setum glacum) and gingilley (Sesamum indicum) are cultivated.

Agro–forestry

He is carrying out agro-forestry practices (late being his old profession) by planting Bamboo, Nelli, Neem, etc.

Horticulture

Sapota, Drumstick, Pappaya, Mango, lime, pome granate are there and getting added every year.

GML: Green Leaf Manure

The GML required is available from his fields, turning to natural manure, reducing chemical manure. Thus, going on friendly with the nature.

Sugar Cane

On an average 3 acres occupy cane which is used for making jaggery. His Labourers are adept (men and women) in converting cane into jaggery. No chemicals are used. Thus, the jaggery remains sound for more than a year. Normally, within a few days the jaggery gets sold like 'hot cakes'. Cane not supplied to cooperative sugar mills where the income is only 50% of jaggery and also there is no knowing when the bills will be settled. Eleven tins of cane juice per time is used in boilerter making jaggery. It takes 50 minutes each time resulting in 200 kgs of jaggery. There will be 6 times such process per day is carried out. For sugarcane crop to be healthier, cane fields should be well aerated; water regime well planned out as per need; no ratmenace, He harvests 35 tonnes of cane per acre.

Paddy

As many as 6 varities are grown Viz, Ponni, Bhavani, Kar, Basmathi, IR 50, Anar Kaly, ASD 19 etc. These are getting sold within 30 days of harvest. The chaff is another supplementing source of income.

Banana

There are 6 varieties of bananas cultivated viz, Robusta, Dwarf, Cavindish etc., Coriander raised during cool months; used for curry leaves and also for fruits. It gives good aroma in its prime for any passer by.

Black gram, green gram, horse gram, red gram are resorted to at appropriate season.

Ground Nut

Ground nut two varieties are grown. Other crops like maize, tapioca are also grown. Yet the list is not exhaustive. The following are also grown, ragi, yamm, backyard, beans, pumkin, lime.

Right thro the year, there is a permanent labour force of ten at work. Thus, ten families are sustained.

Turmeric

Another important crop cultivated by him is turmeric. It is processed and polished in his field itself. Then it is taken to Erode, Salem Markets.

Medical Care

There is a "Medical care programme " where in workers get free treatment from doctors whose monthly bill will be settled by the above farmer. It is interesting to see that the monthly bills don't go above Rs.300.During rainy days, workers are engaged in indoor activities. Yet he has plans to diversify and intensify his schemes. Few are poultry, fishery, dairy etc. Now we may agree from the forgoing that there may not be loss in agriculture in its entirely.

Above all, he is still able to maintain robust health, Which he owes to agriculture which cannot be estimated in terms of money.

PLIGHT OF LANDLESS POOR IN TAMIL NADU

Introduction

Agriculture is the backbone of Indian economy and the prosperity of agriculture is largely responsible for the prosperity of the entire Indian economy. Agriculture sector is contributing nearly half of national income. Agriculture dominates the country's economy to such an extent that 72.05 percentage of working population is dependant on agriculture whereas in developed countries this ratio is very small i.e., in USA 3 percent and UK 8 percent. Mostly, economically and socially backward sections provide agriculture labour. Agricultural labour household is one whose main source of income is wages from agriculture. The agricultural labourers face number of problems in their life and almost all are landless. These landless labourers are attached to the landlords. Due to high growth rate of population, these landless agricultural labourers are bonded labourers. They do not normally receive wages in cash but generally get in kind that too not timely. They have to work for their masters and cannot shift loyalty from one to another. In many cases they have to offer cash, poultry, goats etc. to their unkind masters under coercion. Their employment is based on one-sided contract, with wages determined largely by customs or traditions.

The agricultural labourers are forced to be employed during seasonal periods only and left uncared for, at other times. Their working hours are not fixed; there is no provision for sacred and festival days. Compensatory facilities are not provided by their landlord masters, resulting in poor efficiency, bad health and uncertain life.

Agricultural workers are large in numbers and live in a miserable condition. To ensure a decent living for them it is necessary to understand their plight as hinted above. Their meager wages are far less than needed for a reasonable minimum standard of most tolerant human.

The agricultural labourers are the most exploited and oppressed class in rural hierarchy. They are victims of social discrimination and economic exploitation. By granting of small loans to them, the landlords often succeed in tapping these poor people in their net and converted them into virtual slaves. This slavery continued from generation to generation and forced the agricultural workers to lead to wretched existence of deprivation and oppression. The agricultural labourers are the poorest and "resource less" class in rural areas. Their consumption standards are very low; they are forced to depend on landlords who consequently dictate terms. The simple law of demand and supply operates since they are excessive in relation to the demand for them. They have to settle for extremely low wages. The alternative is unemployment, which is worse. What is their socio economic status and their life style must be the interest of the researchers.

The study of the landless agricultural labours is very important because more people depend on the agriculture. The government has announced many programmes for rural development but they have not reached the landless agricultural labourers. The seasonal employment leads to unemployment. The landless agricultural indebtedness is very high. This study should highlight the plight of the agricultural labourers, which can be used to make policies and welfare activities.

This over dependence of our country on agriculture is a serious weakness of our economy. Hence the study of the socio economic conditions and problems of agricultural labourers require to understand the totality of landless agricultural labourers problems.

It should be one of the primary objects of the five years plans to ensure fuller opportunities for work and better livings to all of the rural community and in particular, to assist agricultural labourers and backward class to come up to the level of rest.

Types of Agricultural Labour in India

Agricultural labour is provided mostly the economically and socially backward sections; poor sections from the tribes as well as their ranks. It may be divided into four types.

(a) Landless labourers who are attached to the landlords.

(b) Landless labourers who are personally independent but who are exclusively for others.

(c) Petty farmers with tiny bits of land who devote most of their time working for others and

(d) Farmers who have economic holding but who have one or more of their children and dependent working for other prosperous farmers.

Magnitude of the Agricultural Labour

According to the second agricultural labour enquiry published in 1960 agricultural labour families constituted nearly 25 percent of rural families. According to this, more than 80 percent of the rural workers are casual, serving any farmer who is willing to engage them only 15 percent of agricultural labourers are attached to specific landlords. More than half of the workers do not possess any land and even the rest of them own only very little of the land. Agricultural labourers predominantly belongs to the scheduled caste, scheduled tribes and other backward classes. According to one estimate, between 75 percent and 80 percent of all agricultural labourers belong to the scheduled caste.

Problems of the Agricultural Labourers

The economic conditions of agricultural workers are very poor and in most of the cases, they are leading a miserable life.

The following are the major problems faced by landless labourers in India.

1. Low wages
2. Low standard of living
3. Indebtedness
4. Adverse working conditions
5. Unemployment and under employment
6. Low per capita income
7. Less annual average expenditure

Present Position of Landless Labourers in India

- The number of agricultural landless labour has increased.
- The days of employment for agricultural abourers have been decreasing.
- The child labour is increasing.
- There is a decline in the wage rate of all type or workers between the two periods.
- Percentage of cash payment of wages is declining making the rural sector more and more demonetized.
- The per capital annual income of the labourers is declining.
- The agricultural labourers are heavily indebted.
- The planning in India between 1950-51 and 1956-1957 has not helped agricultural labourers on the contrary their economic status has deteriorated.

Steps taken by the Government for the improvement of Landless Labourers in India:

1. Minimum Wage Act
2. Indian Constitution and End of Serfdom
3. Organization of Labour Cooperatives
4. Development of cottage industries
5. Stage patronage

Programme

(a) National rural employment programme.

(b) Small farmers development programme or agencies (1970-71),

(c) Integrated rural development porgramme.

(d) Special live stock production programme.

(e) Food for work programme.

(f) Rural landless employment guarantee programme.

(g) Enforcement of minimum wages act'.

(h) Regulation of hours of work.

(i) Provision of social security benefits.

(j) Improvement of better environment.

Suggestions

Irrespective of this landlers poor whether they are reasonable or unreasonable the government should come to their rescue and do things for their upliftment. Being illiterate and not having worldly experience, they are bound be in a depressed mood and we cannot expect wisdom to prevail upon them. I suggest the following for this purpose.

1. A survey should be carried out about their population, which includes both the sexes
2. Literacy among them.
3. Enumeration of houseless and landless among them.

4 In a phased manner, tenements to be built as done in tsunami affected areas.

5. Daily wages from government private institution private bodies to be ensured.
6. Educational institutions near their colony to be enlighten them preferably in the dusk time.
7. Liberal loan to be sanctioned which should be recovered on a long-range programme.
8. Finally, a periodical review to be carried out for further works.

Conclusion

Everyone acquinted with rural conditions in India will agree that the atmosphere prevailing in rural areas is badly affecting the psychology of the labourers. A direct frontal attack is necessary to change these conditions. Take care of the environment and the labourers will take care of himself is a good motto but a better one is to improve at once both the workers and environment so that each may help the other. The environment includes the regulation of work improvement in the conditions of work and provisions of amenities.

ROLE OF YOUTH IN FORESTRY

Every year both state and central Govts are bringing out lot of schemes. Some of those relevant to youth implemented through forestry sector are briefed below.

Wild Life Youth Clubs

Those interested youth of both sex are eligible to join these. There the details of these clubs are appraised to these interested youth. These are both office and field work.

(a) Office Work

For example, "Elephant Study". The youth who become members of the above clubs take six months time in gathering the various available literatures on these giant animals.

(b) Field Work

With this background, they are sent to elephant infested forests to enable to live closely to them, to find out the rate of childbirth; whether it is on the increase or there is a downward trend or it is static. What are their food habits? Is there paucity of their food water and what about the male female ratio? (Normally it should be) what are the diseases and areas available for their unhindered living etc. It is interesting to note where the female ratio increases it results in production of "makhna"(Tusk less males). After this field exercise, the youth have to prepare a project report as to what should be our future elephant management. This is only an example. Such youth are given some concession in the future employment etc. Further details are available with the wild life wing.

Competitions in Schools and Colleges

Every year mostly around wild life week celebrations (First week of October) various competitions viz; essay competition, Elocution competition, Photography, Painting competition, drawing competition etc., are held in educational institutions on behalf forest department.

These are conducted each forest division wise and the winners are rewarded with books, articles, certificates etc., Research studies are given to universities with scholarships. Under NSS Programme huge amounts are allotted to educational instructions by Govt. With a request to spend a portion of the amount on raising nursery and planting works.

Employment Potential

The employment opportunities in forest sector falls under two categories viz; office and field.

(a) Office

The ministerial sector viz, junior assistants, assistants, Superintendents, personal assistants, administrative officers, come under this category. The District Employment officers and the state public service commission sponsor candidates for these.

(b) Field

Reserve watchers, forest guards, foresters, range officers, assistant conservator of forests, and the deputy conservator of forest come under this group. District employment office supplies candidates for the first two categories followed by state public service commission for the next three categories and the last category by the UPSC.

The various educational qualifications; physical requirements; method to apply, whom to apply, when, how, etc., are available with forest department. It is interesting to note here that women also employed as Assistant Conservator of Forests (ACF) and Deputy Conservator of Forests (DCF).

Secret Information

There used to be theft, crimes, Conspiracy for forest wealth. Those youth who give information regarding the above and for proven information these informants are rewarded suitably. There names and identity etc., are kept secret. These informants who are useful in retrieving forest wealth will be considered for employment etc.

Perils in Jobs in Forestry Sector

There is a misapprehension that the field jobs are highly risky. This is not so. The risk in this sector, is like risk in any other sector in Govt Jobs.

I know not even one case of succumbing to this risk of those involved in field works. So it is appealed that with a service mind to the nation youth are welcomed.

Training in Forest Sector

At Vaigai Dam in Theni District Training for Forest Guards and foresters for six months to the farmer and one year for the later category is given. Forest Range Officers get trained at Rangers College at Coimbatore. The above two higher categories are trained at 'Dehra Dun'. The interesting future of training in forest sector is the training is given after recuritement. During training stipend is given.

Publicity

Films are available with forest department depicting maintenance of forests, forest research, wild life, agro-forestry, soil conservation, social forestry etc. These films are taken inland and abroad. There are black and white and colored films. Films of 16mm are common. Films ranging 15 minutes to 2 hours are there. These films are to enlighten youth, workers, public etc. With the forest department, there are projectors, operators, vans etc. The custodian for the state is forest utilization officer. The service is free. One can intend with the respective divisional forest officers also.

Forest Schools

In the tribal areas and in inaccessible areas, forest department runs schools. There are primary schools, high schools and higher secondary schools. In Javadis in TV malai and Vellore districts there are sixteen primary schools and two high schools. These are run as per educational department system and the respective DFO is the DEO. The results in these tribal schools are very much comparable and many times better than the schools elsewhere. The pass percent normally ranges more than 50. These tribal students are adept in sports and there were occasions when these youths represented state in archery particularly. The various buildings, toilets, labs, hostels, quarters for these educational institution are built by forest engineering section. Even there are swimming pools. Normally, there is strength of 300 students. Those passed out are working as doctors, teachers, Post offices and in forest department. The kavadi and mahout (Driver and Cleaner) for the departmental elephants are tribals.

Zoo

The zoo's are now maintained by the forestry sector. The old system of keeping animals in cages for visitors to see is undergoing changes. The animals are kept in open and the visitors are safely kept for viewing them in raised places. The raised places are inaccessible, by these animals. This has gone to the extent of visitors going in cages to view these long-range animals, which is a reverse phenomenon. The visit by youth to this wild life is very much educative. During wild life week celebrations, admission to zoos is free.

Tribals

Tribal form part and parcel of forests. Their living conditions are improving day by day. A visit by youth of this down-trodden people may develop many ideas in them for their upliftment.

Trucking

Trucking routes are made available in the forests. At the start of these places, these are libraries, films and slides etc., The truckers are escorted by forest officials. Herbarium etc, collections can be done enroute. The youth should get experienced in these sorts of thrills.

Forest Fires

Forest Fires are common in summer. Prevention and extinguishing them is major works of this department. There are fires tracing activities to prevent. Youth can volunteer in this venture. So is the case with putting out fires after it has set in. "Fire rewards" are given to adjacent villagers, if adjacent forest areas are prevented from fires. There are fire watchtowers, walkie-talkie equipments. The youths can get engaged in this nation building activities.

Nursery-Forest Nursery in School and Colleges

The saplings required by the forest department can be raised in the above institutions by the youth. The expenditure is borne by the department. These seedlings are taken by the department after paying the dues if any to the youth. Tree planting in schools and colleges; the author is thinking the idea of suggesting every student at the entry stage, to plant a sapling and nurse it till he leaves the institution. By these each institution will have shoals, gardens, parks etc., in them in due course.

A day will come when there will be no place for further planting. It is also suggested, these institution to allot some marks for tree planting activities by the youth. To sum up, it is felt that by engaging the youth in these sorts of national building activities, the terrorist menace will come down; a little contribution by the future generation.

PART - VI
CO-OPERATION

PERFORMANCE OF INDUSTRIAL CO-OPERATIVES IN TAMIL NADU –RECENT TRENDS

Introduction

Village and small–scale industries play an important role in the national economy of India. In a predominently agricultural country like India facing the problem of economic uplift of weaker sectors of the society, the village and small-scale industries play an important role in the national economy.

Those industries have the potentiality to generate income and employment with comparatively small capital investment. India is wedded to the ideal of establishing a socialistic society. It is, therefore, necessary of the community against the exploitation of capitalists and create opportunities for the equalization in the distribution of wealth. This can be achieved though industrial co-operatives. These co-operatives can generate incomes, increase employment opportunities, raise production capacity of the members and help in augmenting their resources though self-help.

The improvement of co-operative industries was first highlighted by the Industrial Commission 1918. The Royal commission on agricultural was also in favour of organising the village artisans on co-operative basis. The Industrial Police Resolution 1956 again stressed the Government intention to develop a steady increasing proportion of the activities of the private sector along co-operative lines.

Working of Industrial Cooperative Societies in Tamil Nadu

Industrial Cooperatives, a wing of the Department of Industries and Commerce, play a vital role;

- In providing gainful employment to the rural people in general and women in particular through production type of industrial cooperative societies.
- In eliminating the exploitation of workers by middlemen through labour contract cooperative societies.
- In arranging for marketing the products of rural artisans through handicrafts cooperative societies.
- In providing infrastructural facilities including developed industrial sites or sheds to the small scale and tiny sector entrepreneurs through Industrial Cooperative Estate.
- In procuring green tea leaves through Cooperative Tea Factories and paying reasonable rate to the small tea growers of Nilgiris District.
- In helping the tapioca cultivators of Salem and Dharmapuri District in procuring the tapioca through member units of sagoserve for processing of starch and sago.
- In sustaining the demand for made Tea in the Nilgiris District in order to ensure reasonable rate to the small tea growers, tea is procured, blended and sold as 'Ooty Tea' through P.D.S. throughout Tamil Nadu by the Indcoserve.
- To stabilize the tea market, and to eliminate the short comings in the conventional tea Auction system, a New Electronic Tea Auction Centre called 'Tea Serve', the first of this kind in the world has been launched and it

transacts sale of tea of 13,44,549 kgs. Per month with perfect to the satisfaction of the tea growers.

In a nutshell, industrial cooperative societies ensure marketing of the finished products of the members, advantages of large-scale economies to the members and mutual help among the members with cardinal principle of each for all and all for each.

Indcosreve Tea Factories

The Indcoserve tea factories were organized with an object of paying a reasonable and remunerative price to the small tea growers for their green tea leaves. Presently, there are 15 Industrial Cooperative Tea Factories with a membership of 19729 functioning in the Nilgiris District. During the period 2003-04, these factories have manufactured 137.46 lakh kgs of made Tea with a sales turnover of Rs. 42.44 crores. Considering the slump in the tea market, the Hon'ble Chief Minister of Tamil Nadu introduced the "Ooty Tea" on 28.8.2001 for distribution of tea through Public Distribution System, so as to stabilize the price of green tea leaves for small tea growers. Under this scheme the Indcoserve purchases made tea from auction centres and marketing it through fair price shops under the control of Registrar of Cooperative Societies and Tamil Nadu Civil Supplies Corporation. Through PDS, 7836.17 metric tonnes of ooty tea worth Rs. 58.77 crores has been sold from the date of inception of this scheme.

In order to eliminate the short comings and deficiencies in the existing conventional auction centres, to ensure transparency in sale of tea through auction and to ensure better price to the Small Tea Growers, a new Electronic Tea Auction Centre at Coonoor under cooperative fold called 'Tea Serve' was inaugurated by the Hon'ble Chief Minister on 13.9.2004. This centre affected a sale of 80.67 lakh kgs. of Tea worth Rs. 26.66 crores upto 31.3.2004.

Sago & Starch

Tapioca is widely grown in Salem and Dharmapuri districts. The small processing units were unble to get a reasonable price for the Sago produced by them and the middlemen exploited them. In order to obtain a remuneration price for the small Sago & Starch units in these districts, a society called sagoserve was established in 1981. Nearly 80% of the national demand for Sago and Starch is being met by the sagoserve. During the period 2003-04, the Sago serve sold starch and sago to the value of Rs. 187.66 crores and earned a net profit of Rs. 2.18 crores. Thus the tapioca cultivators get ready market for their products through the member units of Sagoserve.

Matches

In order to provide marketing support to the small match producers and to protect them from the exploitation of trading companies, match cooperative service societies were organized. There are 7 service societies with a total membership of 372. They provide quality raw materials and other inputs to the members at low prices and undertake marketing of matches in the up country-markets.

Coir

Tamil Nadu stands first in the production of quality brown fibre and is second to kerala in the fibre production. There are 66 Coir Cooperative Societies with activities such as extraction of fibre, production of coir yarn, coir rope, coir mat and mattings and rubberized coir mattresses, pillows. These coir societies provide employment to 1343 persons and have achieved a sales turnover of Rs. 10.32 crores during the period 2003-04.

Handicrafts

Tamil Nadu is famous for many handicrafts items, which are unique in characteristics at international level. The handicraft skill is hereditary and confined mainly to a few families in districts like, Thanjavur, Trichy, Karur and Kanyakumari. In order to protect the Tamilnadu Handicrafts and to improve the economic condition of the craftsmen engaged in this field, this department has organized 20 handicrafts industrial cooperative societies in tamilnadu for providing employment to 369 rural artisans.

Tailoring

With a view to provide employment opportunities to women folk in the rural areas and to the housewives of police personnel in addition to their husband's income, Tailoring Industrial Cooperative Societies have been formed. At present there are 20 tailoring societies, which provide employment to 659 rural women folk and ensures a sizable amount of income to their families.

Engineering

The main object of Engineering type of Cooperative is to provide employment to the skilled workers in the rural areas such as ITI certificate holders, sheet metal workers etc., The production of the society includes locks, bobbins for textile mills, steel almirahs, steel trussers for building etc., The societies also undertake servicing of automobiles, and repairs of furniture etc., There are 11 Engineering Societies which provide employment to 278 persons.

Leather Finishing and Servicing

Finished leather enjoys a very good export market. For providing finishing and servicing facilities to small tanners, societies have been formed. Presently there are two Leather Finishing Industrial Cooperative Societies functioning at Pernampet and Ranipet.]

Cooperative Industrial Estate

The main purpose of forming Industrial Estates under Cooperative fold is to provide work sheds/developed plots, power, water and all other infrastructural facilities and amenities to small and tiny sector industries. The work sheds and developed plots are allotted to the entrepreneurs who are members of the Industries Cooperative estates on hire purchase or out right sale basis. There are 11 Cooperative Industrial Estates in Tamil Nadu with a total membership of 2300 small - scale entrepreneurs.

Labour Contracts

In order to protect the labourers from being exploited by the private contractors, Labour Contract Cooperative Societies were organized for the welfare of the labourers. Presently there are 9 labour contract societies in Tamilnadu, which provides regular employment to 3143 casual labourers ensuring minimum wages, bonus, CPF and other statutory benefits as per the provisions of Labour Act and Factories Act.

Taico Bank

TAICO BANK, established in 1961 caters to the needs of Industrial Cooperative Societies and Small Scale Industries for their financial requirements-presently TAICO bank has 27 branches in the Districts all over Tamilnadu. Now TAICO Back provides jewel loan, personnel loan, housing loan etc to the individual customers. During the period 2003-04, the Bank has mobilised deposits to the tune of Rs.179.64 crores, and sanctioned loans and advances to the tune of Rs. 133.97 crores and earned a profit of Rs. 3.13 crores.

During the past 3 years 43 industrial cooperative societies have been registered. Out of this, 31 societies have commenced their business activities. As on 31.3.2004 there are 318 industrial cooperative societies.

The performance of the societies are as follows :

Year	*No. of Societies*	*Sales Achieved (Rs. in lakhs)*	*No. of Profit Societies*	*No. of Loss Societies*	*No. of Dormant Societies*	*No. of New Societies*	*No. of persons provided with employment*
2001-02	324	34,467.93	158	100	34	32	1,23,382
2002-03	327	28,690.69	175	85	37	30	1,18,685
2003-04	318	33,289.23	182	80	41	15	1,07,408

Conclusion

Therefore, the basic object of all Tamil Nadu Industrial Co-operatives schemes has been to bring about improvement in production, distribution and management techniques for the attainment of the socialist pattern of the society. It could be concluded that all Tamil Nadu industrial co-operatives and catering food services to the society as a whole. In general, general public are also fully satisfied with services rendered by these Tamil Nadu Industrial Co-operative Societies. Hence, Tamil Nadu Industrial Cooperative Societies are playing a very important role in the economic development of Tamil Nadu.

WOMEN EMPOWERMENT THROUGH COOPERATIVE SOCIETIES

Introduction

Cooperation means working together. The principle of cooperation is as old as human Society. It is truly the basis of domestic and social life. Cooperative effort is ultimately the group instinct in man, which enables him to live together and help each other in times of stress and strain. Unconsciously, the principle has always penetrated the life of human race. The history of modern civilization is in fact, the history of cooperation, for without it social and economic progress would have been impossible.

Concept

In the primitive societies the germs of cooperation could be observed in religious institutions and traditional customs. The working of these customs and institutions throw light on the instinct and tradition of mutual assistance, joint possession and joint management, which are found in the thinking and in the life of the people in all ages and all countries. In India, for instance, the principle of cooperation has been practiced from times immemorial. The spirit of village communities of India was almost entirely cooperative. The villages have throughout the ages worked together on an informal corporate basis with regard to their religious and social and cultural life.

In the modern technical sense the genesis of cooperative movement and its applications in the economic field can be traced after the industrial revolution which took place in England during the second half of eighteenth and the first half of the nineteenth century. Today, cooperatives are the most important type of voluntary organization throughout the world. In some countries, they are principal form of organization in agriculture, marketing and provision of credit and distribution of consumer goods. The movement now covers about 98% of the villages and 62% of the total rural population. The caste, color, Religion etc., have not been any bar for the development of the cooperative movement. The working of the cooperative movement all over the world clearly demonstrates that there is hardly any economic need that cannot be met by organizing cooperative societies and hardly any form social or political organization with which they cannot be reconciled or integrated. The cooperative societies have helped to improve security of tenure of land; to consolidate holdings; to promote conservation of natural resources; to facilitate land settlement to foster the all important growth and speed of technical knowledge for better farming to secure savings and administer credit; to reduce the charges made for production requisites and use of the larger capital items for farm and small scale industrial production to reduce charges for consumer goods and services including housing to improve the marketing of farm products to minimize risks and to lower the costs of insurance. They have promoted education both general and vocational. They have provided effective training in democracy and self-government. They have been neither class-bound nor state-bound. They have maintained or increased that sense of interdependence so important for social progress.

Economic and Social Benefits

From the economic stand point, cooperatives are engaged in securing for their members services of various socio-economic activities in the consolidation of holdings, the establishment of irrigation schemes, the contouring of land, the procurement of technical knowledge, the administration credit, the buying of fertilizers, pesticides, seeds, electricity and machine services, of consumers' goods and services, the processing and marketing of produce, the provision of insurance, health and medical care or education. Cooperation has also played an important role in checking monopolistic tendencies.

The social purposes of Cooperation are more diverse than economic purposes. They may be to provide a unique education in democracy, responsibility and toleration to train for political power to evolve an industrial relationship in which the element of authority is much more evenly distributed than in private business to preserve a strong friendly or family spirit and a sense of pride and power which is impersonal to encourage a general advance rather than the advance of particular individuals to secure rational, constructive and unifying approaches to social and economic problems to prevent under-employment to secure the moral as well as the physical satisfaction of pure, quality, correct weight, honest measure, fair dealing in trade or to achieve better physical and mental health. The distinguishing characteristic and social features of Cooperative societies may in many circumstances make these essential to the achievement of their purposes.

Women are not only acting as a primarily obedient daughters, wives and mothers in the society, but also they are acting as Women entrepreneurs in the modern society to make themselves independent and support family in the economic background and to keep social prestige. The rapid growth of women owned business is one of the most important economic developments of recent times. They have started their business at more than twice the rate of men. A majority of women owned business are small retail or service firms and tend to be owned by one person. The areas chosen by women are retail trade, restaurants, hotels, education, cultural, cleaning, insurance and manufacturing. The Cooperatives play an important in uplifting their lives through various schemes.

At present 130 cooperative societies are functioning exclusively for women under the control of social welfare department apart from the schemes like micro credit plan, personal loan, salary loan, entrepreneur loan etc.

A survey, which has been conducted among the women beneficiaries of cooperative sector in Kanyakumari district in this regard; reveals the following. This average age is 45, having different education from school to post graduates, doing various activities like agriculture, business, tailoring and other employment, and the average income is Rs. 40000. They have availed loan under various schemes for women and the average lag in getting loan is 125 days. The average amount taken by them is Rs. 37,500 with the average interest rate of 15%.They have utilized the loan under various purposes like self employment, agriculture, business, family expenditure etc. The impact of getting loan has been analyzed with the help of the following formula by considering the respective items both before and after availing the loan.

The result or impact in getting loan and the utilization of the same lies in the increase in the income and the reflection on increase in the expenditure, assets, home appliances, reduction in the loan and improvement of the standard of living. The survey that has been conducted on studying the impact of loans through cooperatives to women reveals the following. Out of the sample beneficiaries, 94%are able to increase their income, 34%have reduced their loan 56% are able to increase their expenditure pattern, for all the respondents (100%), increase their assets in the way of business, agricultural equipments, land, building and the like are possible, 62% are able to increase their livestock, 86%are able to increase the home appliances like mixie, grinder etc., 52% have shifted their standard of living from low to average, 30% from average to high and 12% from low to high with overall improvement of 94%.

Regarding the attitude of the respondents towards the preference of cooperative banks, they do prefer it mainly because of the easy installment facilities which is followed by the services rendered by them, the prevalence of less formalities, less interest rate, more subsides, counseling they got, training facilities and the availability of more branches.

Conclusion

On an overall assessment, it can be concluded that cooperatives are rendering fruitful services to the society concerned especially to women. The survey reveals that the women are able to enrich their lives. They are fully satisfied with services rendered by these cooperative societies. They got recognition in the society and also economic interdependence in the family. Hence, it is needless to say that cooperatives are playing very important role in the empowerment of women through various schemes.

PART - VII
GENERAL

ALL INDIA SERVICES-PAST, PRESENT AND FUTURE

While every effort has been taken to ensure that there are no mistakes, it is not unlikely that errors might have crept in or omissions gone unnoticed. If any error or omission is noticed, it may be brought to the notice of the Author. Any suggestions for further improvement of this will be gratefully received.

In October 1946, two All India Services, viz., Indian Administrative Service and Indian Police Service, were created to replace the former Indian Civil Service and Indian Police and that the recruitment to these two services should be made through the Federal Public Service Commission on the basis of annual Competitive Examination of a very high standard and that the members of these services should be free from political control, contented and having a sense of security. It was held that by adopting this method the provincial Governments would find the surest means of having an efficient service and maintaining the integrity and impartiality of the members of the services. It was also decided that only a maximum of 25% of superior posts (Cadre posts) should be thrown open to the State Civil/Police Service Officers of outstanding merit as against the maximum of 20% of the superior posts in the ICS/IP.

The above two All India Services were formed and they were put on statutory basis under the Indian Civil Administrative Service Cadre Rules, 1950, the I.P. (Cadre)

Rules, 1950 and the Indian Administrative and Police Services (Pay) Rules, 1950. The All India Services Act, 1951, passed by the parliament, under Article 312(1) of the Constitution of India, empowers the Government of India to make, after consultation with the State Government, rules for the regulation of recruitment and conditions of service of the persons appointment to an All India Service, The All India Services Act, 1951 was amended in 1963 enabling the constitution of the following new All India Services:

(i) The Indian Service of Engineers (Irrigation, Power, Building and Roads);

(ii) The Indian Forest Service; and

(iii) The Indian Medical and Health Service.

The Indian Forest Service has since been constituted with effect from the 1st July , 1966. It has, however, been decided not to constitute the Indian Medical and Health Service and the Indian Service of Engineers (Irrigation, Power, Building and Roads) for the present.

Presently there are 21 cadres each in the Indian Administrative Service, and the Indian Forest Service and 20 in the Indian Police Service. These cadres including the joint cadres of Assam & Meghalaya and of Manipur & Tripura are for the States and one cadre is for the Union Territories. Each cadre, except the cadre for Union Territories is under the control of the state governments concerned. The Union territories Cadres of the IAS and the IPS are under the administrative control of the Government of India in the Ministry of Home Affairs and that of the IFS under the control of the Government of India in the Ministry of Agriculture Irrigation (Department of Agriculture).

The recruitment and the conditions of service of persons appointed to the All India Services are regulated by the rules and the regulations made by the Central Government, in consultation with the State Governments concerned and the

Union Public Service Commission, where necessary, under section 3 of the All India Services Act, 1951. According to the Indian Administrative Service/Indian Police Service (Recruitment) Rules, 1954, framed under the said Act, the ICS and the IP officers have become members of the Indian Administrative Service and the Indian police Service respectively. With the abolition of article 314 of the constitution and the promulgation of the Former Secretary of State Service Officers (Conditions of Service) Act, 1972, their conditions of service have been brought substantially at par with the member of the IAS and IPS. In certain matters the rules and regulations framed under the All India Services Act, 1951 are analogous to those applicable to the Central Services, Group A. This has introduced broad uniformity in the conditions of service of the members of the All India Services wherever they may happen to be serving.

The foregoing has outlined the All India Services in the past and how they have been transformed to present position. In short, the above services from the steel frame of administration. Further more, the Central Administrative Tribunal (CAT) has been specially established to look after the grievances of members of the service even in remote cases where both state govt. and central govt. decides to give penalty for extraneous reasons. While this being the safeguards the members of the service may tend to tow the lines of the political bosses, which was there in the past. But started recently in sporadise manner. This is the reason for some of the AIS Officers are penalized. The blame is partly on the political bosses and partly on the part of the members. For example, the State Govt. may put an AIS Officers in charge of a less important post or some inconvenient postings. To avoid this, temporary difficulties, few of the AIS officers succumb to their political bosses.

It is presumed that this tendency may go on the increase and bring bad name to the entire cadre ultimately bad name to the govt. where they are working.

The short sightedness of the political bosses should not deter these IAS officers and prove their metal and keep up to the expectations of the society, public etc.

References

Indian Civil Administrative Service Cadre Rules, 1950.

The Indian Police (Cadre) Rules, 1950.

The Indian Administrative and Police Services (Pay) Rules, 1950.

The All India Services Act, 1951 Under Article 312 (1) of the Constitution of India.

The Indian Administrative Service/Indian Police Service (Recruitment) Rules, 1954.

The All India Services Act, 1951 Amended in 1963.

The Indian Forest Service Act, 1st July, 1966.

The Former Secretary of State Service Officers (Conditions of Service) Act, 1972.

INFORMATION TECHNOLOGY AND ELECTRONIC COMMERCE

Introduction

The banking sector is in a transitional mode towards a vibrant global market and sophisticated information technology. Due to this changing scenario, banks are paying more attention to expanding their activities from just lending and borrowing to other ends like, insurance merchant banking, leasing, electronic banking etc. Even though these changes were expected after the nationalization of banks in 1969, it was noticed that it had only slow and steady progress necessitating a total revamping of the banking sector. Various reform measures were taken to strengthen the foundation of the system by improving asset quality, enhancing capital and improving profitability along with structural changes in the system. During this transition, banks have seen fierce competition, risk, and revolutionary changes forcing them to take immediate steps to retain market share, redress the grievances of customers as fast as possible by maintaining good ambience, rendering courteous services to customers with the help of latest technological innovations and products.

Globalization and liberalization have forced the banks to think in terms of technology benefits and quality service to customers as future is full of challenges and survival will be a difficult task. The entry of IT infrastructure in the corporate world of banks has brought with it many innovations, in particular the Internet. Though these changes had started with Narasimham Committee's (1992) suggestions for computerization and were followed by Saraf Committee's (1994) recommendations for electronic fund transfers (EFT), Electronic Clearing Services (ECS) and automatic data capture, the banks were actually required to use the BANKET and RBINET and Internet to accommodate itself to the innumerous transactions that had resulted as a result of globalization and liberalization.

The Indian banking industry is not lagging behind, it has started providing services electronically over the internet. These services rendered over electronic media include:

- Phone banking
- ATM–Automatic Teller Machines
- Credit Cards
- Electronic Fund Transfer –EFT
- Shared Payment Network System–SPNS
- Electronic Clearing Service - ECS
- Point of Sale–POS
- D-Mat Accounts
- Electronic Data Interchange
- E-Cheques
- Corporate Banking Terminal

Information Technology

The term "information technology" describes the phenomenon created by the convergence of technologies associated with computing, communication and office systems. In the past, most accounting procedures in banks were paper oriented. With the advent of new techniques like computers, electronic equipments and communication network, the modern accounting system have undergone a sea- change both in their preparation and presentation. The traditional system of preparing the account at quarterly, half yearly and annual lost their relevance since the information are constantly up-dated and made available at any time and anywhere. The information technology enabled the banking organizations to redesign and restructure their functioning.

These services provided by using electronic technology and media are called information technology or electronic banking or e-banking. E-banking has given an opportunity for banks to find solutions to management problems like saving time money and energy or customers by reducing/ minimising paper works, waiting in queues, lack of communication and lack of efficiency. E-banking has provided ease and flexibility in banking operations. The recommendations of Narashimham Committee (1998), for the free and liberal entry of foreign banks in India have further improved the scope for e-banking. As many foreign banks and private sector banks like CITI Bank and ICICI, HDFC banks brought with them IT based products like ATM, credit cards, debit cards, on-line banking etc. This forced the public sector banks and other banks to think on the same lines as these services would help banks to retain their customers, target on banking products and services more effectively to customers.

Customers are also benefited as they are given more free time to indulge in e-commerce business. Therefore, after 1980 throughout the world with majority of banking transactions done through nets or by using information technology. So the information technology solves many problems of the banking industry and very useful to the customers too.

Electronic Commerce

Electronic Commerce has unleashed yet another revolution, which is changing the way businesses buy and sell products and services. It is associated with buying and selling of information, products and services over computer communication networks. E-Commerce helps conduct traditional commerce through new ways of transferring and processing information, since it is information which is at the heart of any commercial activity. Information is electronically transferred from computer to computer, in an automated way. This has, in fact, transformed the way organizations operate.

E-Commerce refers to the paperless exchange of business information using Electronic Data Interchange, Electronic Mail Electronic Bulletin Boards, Electronic Funds Transfer and other net-work-based technologies. It not only automates manual processes and paper transactions, but also helps organizations move to a fully electronic environment and change the way they operate. EDI is still the proven application for E-Commerce, although it is only one of the ways of doing electronic commerce.

Electronic Data Interchange-EDI

EDI refers to the electronic exchange of structure information using telecommunication like payment orders, debits credits, statement of account etc. As part of EDI, satellite communication network is also entering the banks. EDI will very soon do away with branch banking and the customers will identified as ban customer and not branch customer.

EDI can be used to electronically transmit documents such as purchase orders, invoices, shipping notices, receiving advices, and other standard business correspondence between trading partners. EDI can also be use to transmit financial information and payment in electronic form. When used for effecting payments. EDI is usually referred to as Financial EDI and Electronic Funds Transfer (EFT). EDI is a way of substituting electronic transactions for paper ones. EDI allows a new look at the 'processes' within an organization, with a view to reengineer them in what has come to be known as Business Process Reengineering (BPR).

Benefits of EDI

The use of EDI eliminates many of the problems associated with traditional information flow.

1. The delay associated with making documents is eliminated.
2. Since data is not repeatedly keyed, the chances of error are reduced.
3. Time required to re-enter data is saved.
4. As data is not re-entered at each step in the process, labour costs can be reduced.
5. Because time delays are reduced, there is more certainty in information flow.

The other advantage in the use of EDI is that it generates functional acknowledgement whenever an EDI message is received, and it is electronically transmitted to the sender. This acknowledgement states that the message is received.

The EDI message can be immediately processed by the receiving computer without any human intervention, or interpretation or rekeying. Therefore, EDI is most suited in the areas where any of the following characteristics exist:

(a) A large volume of repetitive standard actions
(b) Very tight operating margins
(c) Strong competition requiring significant productivity improvements.
(d) Operational time constraints
(e) Trading partners request for paperless exchange of documents.

Value Added Networks

A VAN is defined as a telecommunication network, primarily for data, that processes or transforms data and information in some way, and thereby provides services beyond simple transport of information.

Electronic Commerce over the Internet

The Internet is an international network of networks. It is a worldwide information highway. It also signifies information resources on innumerable servers on the Net. The Internet allows millions of computers to be linked together offering a global network that connects universities, individuals, government agencies, and now more and more corporate and private enterprises.

EDI was developed for high volume exchange of commercial documents in standardized electronic format between the automated business processes of trading partners. E-mail, on the other hand, is the exchange of less structured correspondence in electronic format.

EC proposes the use of both EDI and E-mail to ensure that the existing barriers to doing business electronically are lowered. EC thus includes any business transacted electronically, whether business-to-business or between a business and its customers. To realize the true benefits, EC is aimed at automating the generation, processing, coordination, distribution, and reconciliation of business transactions. EC is, however, viewed as more than merely automating the manual processes and eliminating paper transactions. It is expected to fundamentally change the way organizations operate.

There are two ways in which EC is being conducted over the Internet. The first is EDI in its present from over the Internet, i.e., the Net is used as a free or cheap network for business communication instead of using the more expensive private VANs. The other is the World Wide Web (www) as a marketplace where vendors can offer goods, information and services for sale and where purchasers can browse, see and feel the goods through browsing tools, before they buy. As a means of distributing public information, the Web has indeed been successful in its goals.

The trend is clear. EDI is growing. The emergence of the Internet and the www has accelerated the development and adoption of EC. Electronic purchasing is increasing, and more and more businesses will use it to transact trade.

Commerce Net

CommerceNet is a consortium of companies, which is promoting the used of Internet for EC. It was launched in 1994 with the aim of creating infrastructure for business-to-business transactions on the Internet. Today, it has over 120 members, which include businesses in financial, retail, education, computer, communication, manufacturing, information services, and publishing fields besides various government and defense agencies.

The objective of CommerceNet is to help companies streamline their procurement and development cycles by performing transactions online.

EDI and EC will change the way business and commerce are conducted. Electronic documents will substitute paper documents. Proprietary VANs on which EDI messages are exchanged will give way to the Internet, which is more cost effective. Issues relating to security of transactions, confidentiality of messages and integrity of data are central to trade and financial payments. These are being addressed to make Internet commerce more reliable and acceptable in the marketplace.

Application of Information Technology

Phone Banking

Bank on phone, provides easy access for customers to have large businesses through telephones. Data are exchanged over the phone regarding any queries, to issue instructions on balance transfer, statement of account, cheque book, stop payments, new schemes, interest rates etc. at any convenient time and place. Telebanking has gone a long way in providing maximum customer satisfaction within the limited infrastructure.

Automatic Teller Machines: (ATM)

Banks in the cities to provide cash dispensation to their customers around the clock install ATMs. Now, the banks provide this facility in a more sophisticated way that a customer of one bank and branch can withdraw from any other banks, at any other branch, nation wide. In developed countries, this service is provided to their blue chip client globally. This is possible only through worldwide networking and communication system.

Credit Cards

These plastic cards enable customers to spend whenever he/she wants within the prescribed limits and pay later. Debit card is a prepaid card with stored value, whereas credit card is post paid with fixed limits. It is seen that spending is higher through debit cards than with credit cards currently CITY Bank and time bank have started with Debit cards and now other banks are also following these to launch their own cards.

Electronic Funds Transfer: (EFT)

Electronic funds transfer is a system of processing and communication of payment through el4ectronic methods. EFT assumes greater significance in the banking system as the RBI also encourages the commercial banks to adopt this technique. Inter and intra bank transfers of funds are now made through this EFT mechanism. Transactions of high value i.e., at least more than one lakh is now made through this cost effective and quick system of settlement. Normally, payments are made through cash, cheques, drafts and credit cards. The latest in this process are the debit card system, charge, digital cash, electronic purse and so on.

SPNS- Shared payment network system

SPNS installed by the IBA in the city of Mumbai, enables electronic banking service like cash transactions, extended hours of banking, utility payments, cheques, point of sale facilities by the SPNS can go to any ATM linked to SPNS.

Electronic Clearing Services [ECS]

Electronic clearing of funds from one centre to another for handling bulk transactions like salary, interest, dividend, commission etc., has dispensed the cheques. A part of electronic clearing service is computerized clearing of cheques at metropolitan centers and linking with international communication system of SWIFT. These services have contributed in a great way towards improving the customer services globally. ECS was introduced in India in 1996. It has made it possible for customers to get the funds next day itself.

Point of sale [POS] terminal

Payment card at a retail location for electronic transfer of fund is called POS. The client enters his personal identification number [PIN] and confirms the amount due. Customer's account is automatically debited with the amount of purchases and it credits the retailers account POS installed at petrol stations and large retail houses are linked to banks network.

D-Mat Accounts

Transacting shares business through electronic media is called D-Mat. Investor opens an account called Demat Accounts with DPS. They get shares in electronic form.. Then they send the actual shares to the investor. Investor pays for the opening, maintenance and collection of shares. This has reduced the paper work, bad deliveries; loss of shares and less transaction cost. However delays in demating, higher cost charged by the investors has not given a good start for the growth and scope of Demat in India. Depository participant sometimes make illegal money at the cost of investors. SEBI should find ways to over come this to give a good scope for Demat in India.

Electronic Data Interchange-EDI

EDI refers to the electronic exchange of structure information using telecommunication like payment orders, debits credits, statement of account etc. As part of EDI, satellite communication network is also entering the banks. EDI will very soon do away with branch banking and the customers will identified as ban customer and not branch customer.

E-cheques

Digital cheque used by the payer to the payee through internet is called e-cheques. Electronic versions of cheques are issued, received and processed. Most of the banks use e-cheques. A secure means of operation is provided for collecting, payments, and transferring cash flows through this method. The payer issues a digital cheque to the payee and the entire transactions are done through internet.

Computerised Accounting

Development in computer has brought about a change in the accounting practices in banks. A wide range of software packages were developed recently, which attributed to the widespread use of computers to increase the information needs. Microcomputer are used to keep records and for processing. Microcomputer is small unit capable of doing calculations, storing data and programmers. These computer range from small personal computer (PCs) to a blue chip "dest top" business computer. The microcomputers are used for word processing, spreadsheet application etc. if the computer is not properly used, and it will result in unfair accounting and loss of information. However, computer provides better information and increases the effiency of the banks.

Data base with different technology such as lost terminal, file server and client server system established all over the world. For creation, manipulation and share information, tools such as Microsoft windows were developed and applied. This Microsoft windows provide graphical user interface, window based word processing along with window based spreadsheet and E-mail package. Information technology now uses geographic information system (GIS) and global positioning system (GPS).

GIS means type in a map to any other type of data. GIS is capable of converting data into pictures and graphs.

GPS means the system, which enabled the precise navigation and targeting of many of the weapons used during the gulf war.

E-Mail

The system of sending messages from one computer to another is known as "E-mail. E-mail originally was introduced in the year 1983 in U.S.A. to send the messages through E-mail, a mini personal computer, one telephone line, a modern and software support is required. Modern is of various types like kotex, robotex, multi-moderna etc. the change for sending a message with 250 characters (bits) through E-mail is Rs. 2. for express it is Rs. 4. for foreign countries it is Rs.15 per page. If it is sent through telex or fax it costs Rs. 5 extra for transmission even within our country.

There are different commands like read mail, prepare mail, mail list, status, message forward etc. each of these commands do different functions for example, read mail enables us to read the message sent by other to our computer.

From the above we can understand that E-mail is the most economical and confidential mode of transmission of information globally.

RBI Net: (RBI NET)

This scheme facilitates the transfer of funds by a customer former any bank, any branch, any center to his client at some other center, so other bank and/or branch. Settlements between banks and with the RBI are now a day done through this system. Inter and tntra bank clearing are also done through this electronic communication system.

Internet

Internet is a system interconnected with network worldwide. The increasing popularity of the Internet is the worldwide web (WWW), which connects millions of servers. In India there are 500 Internet hosts nd more than 750 web sites that provide this Internet service. The Internet has 25 million computer buffs and their population explodes at a rate of 10% per month. Internet has found a nest off 150 countries. Arpanet developed by the USA in 1969 was the base for this magical development of Internet. Only those who master the computer commands can work successfully on the Internet.

The Internet has many features. E-mail is one of the simplest facilities available on the Internet. Through this Internet, a subscriber can set up a newsletter, or a discussion through which the participants exchange their views. In the modern age, it is possible to transmit texts; pictures and voices information from anywhere, in any form in the world is accessible to the subscriber at the press of a button and at a very minimum cost.

Computer on the Internet communicate with each other in a number of ways. These methods are called services. The most popular services are:

1. Worldwide web
2. E-mail
3. FTP (file transfer protocol)
4. Use net news

5. ERNET
6. Browser
7. Graphic Viewers
8. New Reader
9. Uniform Resource Locator (URL)
10. Hypertext Transfer Protocol (http)
11. Gopher News
12. Wide Area Information Service (WAIS)
13. Application of information Technology in the Banking System

The following are the specific Areas where information technology can be used in the banking system.

(i) Preparation and posting in ledger (LAN)

(ii) Portfolio management (genetic algorithm)

(iii) Funds management and transfer (on-line banking)

(iv) Credit appraisal

(v) Foreign exchange transaction

(vi) Opening of letter of credit

(vii) Issue of letter of guarantee

(viii) Decision making at senior manager level

(ix) Employees training and education

(x) Preparation and submission of financial statements

(xi) Identification of fraudulent credit card transactions (neutral network system)

Benefits

The information technology can be administered in the banking system. The application of information technology will help in increasing the operating efficiency of the banking system. Its application will result in saving in cost. The quality of the information can be improved. The branches can provide improved customer services. This will enable the domestic banks to face and challenge the competition from their foreign rivals. There will be a reduction in the staff strength to a considerable extent due to the adoption of information technology. The working condition of the bank branches can be improved.

Benefits of E-Banking Services

- It reduces cost of both in services and administration.
- Overcoming the geographical barriers.
- Cost minimized for customers.
- It helps to maintain customer loyalty.
- Web site enable banks to develop advertisement.
- Information technology enable banks to deliver products and services.
- Multimedia capabilities offer homogenous branding.
- Online banking encourages promotion of various schemes of the bank.
- Individualized and customized services with the help of integrated customer data.
- Minimizing fraud and misappropriation by inter-branch reconciliation.
- Convenience to customers–like card free banking, cash free banking provides a domain of access to banking services.

Reasons for Poor Achievement

1. Poor initial introduction of the information technology concepts in the banks.
2. Improper implementation of techniques of information technology.
3. Improper selection of hardware and software will result in heavy cost and inefficiency.

4. Inadequate suppliers support after the purchase of the IT system.
5. Fear and reluctance among the staff regarding reduction of staff followed by retrenchment due to the introduction of information technology.
6. Brain drain is yet another cause for the poor implementation of the information technology.
7. Lack of co-ordination between the management and staff is another reason for the poor achievement.

Conclusion

The current trends are quite comforting for customer-but it does pose threats and problems to banks. As we find information technology invading the banking sector, only banks, which used the right technology could come out with success. Banks are required to 'restructure', re-invent and reengineer themselves go meet the necessary performance improvement and get the competitive edge due to the introduction of information technology (e-banking) being an important out pout of ;information technology has ushered in an era which is transforming the entire functioning of banks. The tilt in the banks from traditional to modern e-banking services has been welcomed due its advantages, but banks in India are taking time to get rooted. Banks are slow but are going to offer in further more e-banking services to keep in pace with the evolving pattern of customers demand.

The flexibility of e-banking offers unprecedented opportunities for the bank to reach out to its customers. With the rapid expansion of the Internet facilities, e-banking is all set to play a very important role in the 21st century. Banks have to deal with the sophisticated clientele with the help of latest technology like e-banking. Lack of coordination and cyber crimes encroaching. E banking if taken in the right way by banks and customers would take the economy to its best and make it a boon to customers.

Introduction and/or development of information technology will not only affect the banking system of our country but the entire banking system of the world. It is high time to advise and train the banking personnel on the acquisition, installation and use of the information technology. Though there was a cry against the introduction of information technology, it is better to adopt it to face the stiff competition from the ever-dynamic foreign counterpart. As the banks become more sophisticated, the benefits of information technology will grow into leaps and bounds. Further research may be conducted on the feasibility of the introduction of home banking, mobile ATM, office banking, phone banking edger payment system and so on.

References

G.S. Mongia, R.K. Sinha, Nationalisation of Banks Retrospect and Prospects.

R.V. Kulkarni, B.L. Desai, Knowledge based system on Banking Sector.

I.V. Trivedi, Indian Banking in the new millennium.

M.P. Jaiswal, Anjali Kaushik, e-CRM-Business System frontiers.

C.S. Rayudu –E-Commerce, E-Business.

E-Commerce-S. Pankaj.

Developing Accounting: Point Publishers, Jaipur 2004, p. 489-493.

Journal of Accounting and Finance: Vol. vii, No. 1, Spring 2004 p.14-24.

Journal of Accounting and Finance: Vol. ix, No. 1, Spring 2004, p. 76–89.

Banking finance: Vol vii, No. 7, July 2003, p. 3-4.

Indian Overseas Bank Quarterly News Review: Vol vii, No. 1, Jan-March 2004, p. 10-12.

Punjab National Bank Monthly Review: July, 2003, p. 346-353.

The Week: 17 Sep. 2003, p. 28 & 29.

The Banker: Sept. 2004, p. 20.

Information Communication World: Oct. 2004, p. 11-14.
SBI Monthly Review: Oct. 2003, p. 521-527.
Harari, Liat and Dalit Tzafrir, Electronic Commerce.
Mong Le, Thao, The Beauty of Internet.
Computers Today, June, 2004.
EC World, June, 2004.
EC World, July, 2005.

MOVE WITH THE WORLD–CHANGES IMMINENT INCOMMERCE EDUCATION AND CURRICULUM

The stereo-typed system of limiting our knowledge to books alone for the last 50 years will not deliver the goods any more. In the changing world lot of practical difficulties have erupted in, which has no salvage in the above system. So the stereo-typed system should accommodate the prevailing and future such practical difficulties, without which in course of time there will be no takers for this, except the captive audience. It is paining to see that the old commerce curriculum is going on unmindful of the changing world.

There should be proportionate changes in the commerce curriculum to commensurate with the competition of the modern world. What is going on through the class-room demonstration today? Students are given only theoretical education and not even an iota of practical aspects. For instance, An automobile engineer traveled in his car driven by his driver who do not have full knowledge of the functioning of car. Whereas the engineer not knowing driving as knowledge of the functioning of car. The owner had to be at the service and benevolence of the driver since he has only theoretical knowledge of car mechanism.

This is the sort of affairs between theoretical and practical education. Therefore, commerce curriculum should now be mostly practical oriented. In the present day competitive world, educational system should be modernized in tune with the fast moving and changing world.

Commerce Education is the backbone of the business field. The success in the business depends upon the quality of manpower etc. utilized. Commerce Education should keep phase with changing trends.

Commerce Education has a crucial role in our society including various political parties, religious organizations; where expertise in commercial knowledge is required. The commerce degrees are intended for acquiring a conceptual knowledge and managerial skills in the wide spectrum, of business and Industry. Today's highly developed industrial, commercial and business world requires highly qualified and cute commerce graduates. Hence it is inescapable to shape and mould the commerce students to suit the global changes.

Education is a medium through which knowledge and intelligence required by individual or society can be obtained or properly formulated. Commerce begins with functional aspect and then leads to liberal or ideological aspect. The individual and the society get goods and services at the doorsteps. The commerce system deals every part of human life and thus commerce education becomes an education for better living. The close relationship between the functions of syllabus and socio-economic development and cultural values has led to the increasing realization of the importance of syllabus formation. So we must introduce vocationalization concept in commerce as recommended in1882 by Hunter's commission to have two types of curriculum namely subjects for higher studies and vocational and practical subjects. It was Gandhiji's Nai Tamil (1936), which conceived education as an independent stream with training to prepare students for identified occupation.

Present world is characterized by fast changing conditions of demand and technology. There will be much uncertainty than in the past. Our research and development organization will have to acquire, and adapt latest technologies in improving the quality and so as to stay in the competitive world.

The world is changing very fast. The speed of LPG has tremendously influenced the various dimensions of commerce education. Most of the scholars are recommending to re-orient the commerce course. Present syllabi of all universities are not able to meet the different types of challenges posed by industry and business. There are no practical orientation to develop skills and qualities among youngsters. Thus there is a need for reorienting and restructuring commerce education by introducing uniform syllabi at the national level. Most of the colleges and even few universities have not recognized the importance of IT and IT related skills. Therefore, students are not getting opportunity to acquaint themselves with tools of information technology. The professional bodies, Trade Associations, Chambers of Commerce have shown very little preference to associated universities in redesigning the commerce courses.

"India is rich in resources; culture and education too." It is right time to enrich us not only with basic curriculum but also in modernized infrastructure facilities. By this way, we can minimize our Indian students migrating to foreign countries for quality education. There is a need for globalization of education too, to face the competitions from foreign Universities and in ensuring quality education with placement.

Our country is positioning in the global economy, where the world has predominantly become interdependent in terms of trade, culture and communication. However some institutions in India are competing on par with the world-class education. The knowledge of state of commerce is expanding and diversifying. As social culture shifts from ideal to material, commerce education has shifted moving from abstract thinking to thoughtful action, perceptions and practices gaining prominence. In view of changes in the objectives of education the commerce discipline should enter the system of general education right from secondary stage. As far as India is concerned, commercial sciences must find their place in higher education specially to achieve following goals of education.

Development of total integrated personality of the student; Commitment to society through involvements in development programmes and actions; Application of new methods of Science and Technology effectively in line with industry and agriculture; Improving productivity of human efforts towards improving quality of life and Entrepreneurisation of the society.

In Commerce, transportation of goods from one place to another is unavoidable. In the past, transporting commodities was expensive; time consuming and risky. Therefore commerce was restricted mainly to local markets. With the advancement of technology in transportation commerce expanded considerably. Today commerce takes place between neighboring households; between neighboring cities; and between neighboring countries by International shipping, mail services, and advancement in information technology; Internet; enables commerce among people from any location in the world.

Industrial growth affected commerce in a verity of ways and a revolution has taken place in land transportation. There were trade barriers, and depressions in some parts of the world, due to fury of nature, war between countries; internal political and economic set backs. These have retarded commerce growth. Series of international conferences and discussions between member countries slowly but steadily dismantle many of the restrictions though not completely. With the execution of General Agreement on Tariffs and Trade (GATT) and the formation of customs unions, like European

Union, have brought about a significant reduction in tariff reductions.

With the explosive growth in Electronic Commerce, referred in general as E-Commerce, there was spurt in the growth of commerce, world over E-Commerce follows the same basic principles that traditional commerce follows-that is, buyers and sellers exchange and transport goods from one place to another. But in e-commerce the exchange is facilitated by network computers. Buyers order goods and services online.

They track the status of their order in electronic mail, and in some cases, they receive the goods they purchase directly over the Internet. Computer software, digital music and video, online information, and other products and services can all be distributed in electronic formats. In cases, products ordered online are delivered using traditional shipping methods.

At the close of the 20th century, retail transactions made up the largest part of e-commerce. Consumers purchased computers, airline tickets, hotel rooms, automobiles, clothing, electronic, books, even tickets, food, furniture, and countless other commodities over the Internet.

Having seen the development in the field of commerce World over, India being Developing Nation with rich human resources and being predominantly an agricultural country, with phenomenal potential in Accounting, legal and electronic fields, it is necessary to make an introspection in educational system and the curriculum. So that India is not out of the race. There is a disturbing statistics over the number of students who go abroad to study and it is increasing in an alarming proposition. It was told that in 2003 there were 3,03,000 international student enrolments in Australia. There is also a substantial growth in the courses and degrees and diplomas offered by foreign universities and they lure the student community.

Why is there this migration and what is needed in our system of education to meet the international standards should be addressed with top most priority. I am sure fruitful discussion will bring about meaningful suggestion to restructure the corporate curriculum.

Views

- A student of Today's world is well informated. He selects an Institution and for that matter even the Nation, which imparts the knowledge, based on variety of reasons; the Institutions reputation; a excellence in education and of the fastest growing segments of e-commerce. Businessess ordered supplies and coordinate training, safety and stability of the society of country, the high standard of living that exists, to name a few.
- An educational system should reflect quality, excellence and innovation. We should create vast exciting and ever evolving educational opportunities, to facilitate students to realize their potential in ways that they have planned and perhaps in ways that they would not have imagined. If we have to compete, our educational institutions should impart the most modern skills cost effectively through innovative teaching, by providing best infrastructures and facilites, and welcoming a multicultural society enjoying a quality life style in a safe environment.
- There is an urgent need to introduce a vast range of courses including traditional academic areas of learning and research, as well as more practical courses with a vocational orientation. It is necessary that the courses should be designed in such a way that more importance is placed in developing the ability of students to think creatively and independently, read widely and critically participate in seminars, debates, workshop and function as a team. The end users need should be borne in mind

and the above said attributes are those, which the present day Employers look for.

- The other area that needs attention is the Educational institutions should meet high standards of quality and ethical practices. These standards should apply equally to public and private institutions and centers. Various issues like, curriculum, teaching staff qualifications, constant programmes to update their knowledge and facilities offered should be constantly reviewed. Every instruction should have their own code of conduct and set standards for academic and support services. There should be a commitment to quality, education and training and these should be provided at affordable costs, without compromising on quality. All efforts should be taken to enter into collaborative agreements with other institutions exchange of professional skills, which will provide a competitive edge in providing world-class education and training.
- For an example, Australia, a place, where the system of education and institutions are ranked as best in the world, have as many as 4500 agreements with other institutions around the world.
- It is necessary to identify the core competence and provide the students community all that they need to face the challenges in the present world of stiff competition, where the fittest alone will survive. It is also necessary to have the courses designed to meet the needs of the Industry and the captains of Industry. There is an urgent need to depart from the traditional method of testing the competence of the students by three hour long written examinations, where mostly the memory alone is tested rather than the in-depth knowledge of the student on the subject. It is true that a strong foundation about the fundamentals is important, but in the end the student should be moulded to face the commercial world.

Suggestions

- In the three-year commerce courses, be it accounting corporate Secretary ship or business administration, the first year should essentially concentrate on the fundamentals, i.e.the substantive Portion, and the second year should be more application orinted, this could be by way of presenting a problem before the participants in Groups, and triggering their creativity and watching how they approach the problem. This will enhance their communication skills, leadership qualities and will provide an overall personality development. The third year should concentrate on project work.
- The two-year masters degree viz.: post graduate Degree, should focus on the advanced level of the subjects as required nationally and internationally. This exposure should facilitate the students to proceed further to do research on the subject of his choice.
- There should be courses designed to bridge the gap between the captains of the industry and the professionals. A short duration course on business laws, drafting and conveyance will be a right choice.
- The need of the hour should be studied and courses designed rather than concentrating on traditional courses. Insurance business is on the card, arbitration laws, international laws, E-governance, Global accounting standards and practices, corporate restructuring, how to read a balance sheet. Corporate governance, are few more areas where one year certificate or diploma courses could be designed both for the students and the company executives.
- There should be compulsory programmers for the faculties to get themselves acquainted with the latest developments and changes and applications. There should be continuous exchange of programmes between institutions to share the knowledge and expertise.

- The students should be exposed to basic computer knowledge and it should form part of the curriculum basic packages like TALLY.
- More opportunities should be provided for the students to exhibit their skills, by organizing frequent one-day students' programs, competitions, quiz both within the college and inter college events. There should be a quarterly journal which can be called as a newsletter, wherein the students would be encouraged to make their presentations in the form of articals, write ups etc.,
- Executives of various companies could be invited to deliver lectures at frequent intervals, to share their practical knowledge and exposure. Ultimately the success lies in putting the theories so learnt into practice.

MUTUAL FUND INDUSTRY IN INDIA

Economic Scenario

The world economic scenario in 2004-05 witnessed a new dimension. The U.S. economy remained under pressure, while India and china emerged as dominating forces. The Indian capital market witnessed many ups and downs during the period under review. When the UPA Government took over the charge in April\May 2004 with the support of left parties, uncertainity prevailed about the continuation of the reform process, which was initiated by the previous Government. On 17th May 2004, the BSE Sensex fell more than 800 points in a single day transaction. SEBI had to intervene to close the stock market for sometime to avoid further fall. However, clarifications issued by Government and left parties thereafter and further positive steps taken by the Government to improve the economy restored confidence and the market has boomed thereafter. It almost touched the level of 7000 in March 2005. This unprecedented move in the capital market on account of economic growth, rationalization of the tax structures, better exports, improvement in the corporate results is commendable inspite of rise in the international crude price.

India is likely to remain among the fast growing economies in the world in the medium term. A strong pick up in the activities in the industrial and services sector helped to sustain growth in FY 2005 despite some weakness in the agriculture sector. While service sector continues to remain the backbone of growth, the resurgence of the industrial sector increased business optimism and consumer confidence, thus creating an improved investment climate. India now appears to be the midst of another investment climate. India now appears to be the midst of another investment cycle, supported by a strong capex cycle and emphasis on infrastructure development.

Mutual Fund Industry-At A Glance

Financial year 2005 was definitely a year with a difference for the Mutual Fund industry. During the year, 97 new schemes were launched and more than Rs. 25000 crs. was mobilized from the market. This is a record by itself, which indicates that confidence of the investors in mutual funds is increasing.

The Indian Mutual Fund industry still to organize systems to adequately mobilize investments from semi-urban and rural areas. Efforts need to be capture this growing income source and generate interest in the minds of investors from the rural and semi-urban areas. The fact is that unitholders of most of the Funds are currently either corporate investors or high net worth investors of big-cities. It is a paradoxical situation that the special purpose vehicle, which was designed for the small and retail investor has been effectively utilized by the larger corporates/investors.

Though industry is showing robust growth, it still has a challenge before it-a challenge to reach out to retail investors and to position the Mutual Fund products as long-term investment avenues for the household sector. More innovative schemes including those offering sophisticated products need to be designed.

Performance of Taurus Mutual Fund-the Year in Retrospect

At present Taurus mutual fund is managing following six open-end schemes:

Equity oriented schemes

- The Starshare
- Discovery Stock Fund
- Bonanza Exclusive Growth Scheme

Equity Linked Saving Schemes

- Libra Tax Shield

Income Schemes

- Libra Bond Fund
- Libra Gilt Fund

It is heartening to report that performance of all the schemes has shown considerable improvement during the period under review. This year has been utilized for consolidating the business as well as restructuring and rebalancing the portfolios of all the schemes. Such proactive approach in our investment strategy helped to improve the NAVs of all the equity schemes. Our efforts will be to remain a leader in performance inspite of our small size. This itself will be a big challenge.

After a successful closure of Fixed Maturity plan-1 under Libra Bond Fund, FMP-II was launched in September/ October 2004.

Performance of the Schemes

The performance of individual schemes during the year is reviewed hereunder:

Starshare

NAV on 31.03.04	*NAV on 31.03.05*	*% age of change*	*BSE 200 on 31.03.04*	*BSE 200 on 31.03.2005*	*% age of change*
10.89	18.86	73.19	733.53	867.58	18.27

This is an open-end equity growth scheme with the objective to provide long term capital appreciation. The scheme has generated more than 70% return during the Financial Year 2005 Whereas BSE-200,which is being used as the benchmark index to evaluate the performance of equity schemes, has moved up by 18.27% only. BSE-30 Sensex has moved 16.14% only. During this period, NAV of the scheme has improved from Rs.10.89 per unit to Rs.18.86 per unit as on 31st March 2005.

During this period, market has shown more resilence towards midcap stocks. Since portfolio of the scheme is titled towards midcap stocks, upswing in the NAV was quite evident. With the restructuring of the portfolio, investors' confidence is building up which is now reflected from the fresh inflows in the scheme.

We have also changed the Investment Policy for the scheme and now the entire portfolio is divided in:

(a) Investment for long term purpose

(b) Investment for short and medium term purpose.

Keeping this policy in mind, about 20% - 30% of the assets of the scheme are being invested for long-term purpose and balance for short-term purpose. Profit looking is now being done on regular basis and funds are reinvested in the market to generate better returns.

With the improvement in the capital market and portfolio restructuring, the percentage of liquid equity shares has also come down to 0.91% from 3% of the NAV during this year.

Discovery Stock Fund

NAV on 31.03.04	*NAV on 31.03.05*	*% age of change*	*BSE 200 on 31.03.04*	*BSE 200 on 31.03.2005*	*% age of change*
5.67	9.53	68.08	733.53	867.58	18.27

Initially, the scheme was launched as Newshare scheme in 1994 as a close end scheme. The scheme was, however, converted into open end in March 2000 and name was changed from New share to discovery Stock Fund.

The investment objective of the scheme is to identify and select low priced stocks through discovery mechanism, which would include:

(i) Undervalued stocks offering opportunities for growth potential.

(ii) Low priced stocks with decent dividend yield

(iii) Stocks where lower side risk is minimum

(iv) Stocks of turnaround cases with potential for improvement.

This scheme has also shown considerable improvement during the financial year 2004-2005. The scheme has given a return of more than 68% during the period under review, whereas BSE-200, which is being used as the benchmark index to evaluate the performance of equity schemes, has moved up by 18.27% only. BSE-30 Sensex has moved up by 16.14% only. The NAV has improved from Rs. 5.67 per unit as on 31st March 2004 to Rs. 9.53 per unit as on 31st March 2005. The portfolio is being regularly monitored and restructured depending upon the sector performance. we hope that performance of the scheme will improve further in the current year.

This scheme was taken over from Bank of India Mutual Fund in March 2002. This is also an equity oriented growth scheme, the objective being long- term capital appreciation. When this scheme was taken over from Bank of India, the NAV was Rs. 9.18 per unit as on March 23,2002. Portfolio of the scheme has been restructured with more thrust on the front line stocks and the present portfolio mainly consists of active and fundamentally strong stocks. In this scheme, percentage of mid cap stocks is less, therefore, NAV has moved up by about 25%,which is more in tandem with the BSE-200,the benchmark index, which moved by 18.27%, during the period under review. The entire investment in the scheme is highly liquid and scheme does not carry any illiquid stock.

Bonanza Exclusive Growth Scheme-open

NAV on 31.03.04	*NAV on 31.03.05*	*% age of change*	*BSE 200 on 31.03.04*	*BSE 200 on 31.03.2005*	*% age of change*
14.63	18.26	24.81	733.53	867.58	18.27

NAV of the scheme has moved up from Rs. 14.63 per unit as on 31st march 2004 to Rs. 18.26 per unit as on 31st March 2005.

As such, the performance of the scheme is satisfactory.

Libra Tax Shield

NAV on 31.03.04	*NAV on 31.03.05*	*% age of change*	*BSE 200 on 31.03.04*	*BSE 200 on 31.03.2005*	*% age of change*
9.75	15.64	60.41	733.53	867.58	18.27

Libra Tax shield is an open-end equity linked tax saving scheme with endeavor to provide tax benefit and long term capital appreciation by investing in a portfolio of equity and equity-linked securities. Being a tax saving scheme, there is a lock in period of 3 years from the date of investment.

In terms of the Finance Act 2005, section 88 of Income Tax Act 1961 has been modified as section 80C whereby investment upto Rs. 1 lac in Libra Tax Shield will be eligible for deduction U/S 80C for assessment year 2006-07 and subsequent years.

With this modification in the income tax rule, Libra Tax Shield can now be treated at par with the other available tax saving instruments in the market where average returns vary between 6% to 8% p.a. only.

During the financial year 2003-2004, total dividend of 27% was declared in the scheme. The Net asset value of the scheme has also improved from Rs. 9.75 per unit as on 31st march 2004 to Rs. 15.64 per unit as on 31st March 2005.

Further, the dividend distributed by the scheme is exempt from tax in the hands of the investors and investment in the scheme is also exempted from wealth tax. As the investment is locked in for a period of 3 years from the date of investment, no capital gain tax is applicable at the time of redemption.

The scheme has given a return of more than 60% in the financial year 2004-05 inspite of its low corpus.

There is no illiquid security in the scheme. For the benefit of the small investors, Systematic Investment Plan (SIP) has been introduced in this scheme whereby unitholder can invest fixed sum of rupees every month or every quarter by purchasing additional units of the scheme at the applicable NAV.

Libra Bond Fund

NAV on 31.03.04	*NAV on 31.03.2005*	*% age of change*	*Crisil Composite bond fund index on 31.03.05*	*Crisil composite bond fund index on 31.03.05*	*% age of change*
12.1167	13.3979	10.57	1206.78	1208.99	0.18

The scheme was launched in July, 2001 as an open-end bond scheme with investment objective to maximize income through a basket of dept, bonds, debentures, Government securities and money market instruments etc. of varying maturities while maintaining safety and liquidity.

In this scheme, there are two options for the investors

- Growth Option
- Dividend Option.

The scheme was consistently performed satisfactorily except during certain periods when there were big falls in the bond market.

The initial investment strategy adopted was to invest in securities of long-term maturity, which was later reduced to medium term maturity securities. With more funds coming into the scheme, the strategy is expected to be towards investment in securities of short term, medium and long term maturities so as to maximize returns for the investors.

During the year, Fixed Maturity Plan (FMP-I) launched under the scheme was matured on July 1, 2004. Thereafter, FMP-II was launched on September 3, 2004. The performance of FMP-II is also satisfactory.

During the year, average return in both the options i.e Growth and Dividend, was more than 10% whereas Crisil Bond Fund Index has moved upward only by 0.18%

Libra Gilt Fund

NAV on 31.03.04	*NAV on 31.03.2005*	*% age of change*	I-sec *composite index on 31.03.05*	*Crisil composite index on 31.03.05*	*% age of change*
12.6307	12.9451	2.49	3432.52	3423.64	(0.26)

The scheme was launched in July 2001 as an open-end gilt scheme with investment objective to provide risk free returns to investors through investment in securities issued by central Government or State Governments or any security unconditionally guaranteed by Government of India.

In this scheme, there are two options for the investors

- Growth option
- Dividend option.

The scheme has performed satisfactorily during the year except during certain periods due to volatility in the government securities market.

The investment strategy during the year in the scheme had been to invest in medium to long-term securities and that had yielded good results. However, the investment approach will be flexible so as to maximize returns for the investors. The scheme was launched as No-load scheme.

Libra Leap and bonanza equity linked saving on tax scheme 1993-Redeemed Schemes

Libra Leap scheme and Bonanza Equity saving on Tax scheme 1993 were pre-maturely redeemed in October 2002. Unit holders who have not yet applied for redemption are being periodically reminded to surrender unit certificates/ transaction slips for claiming redemption proceeds. Funds still lying with us in respect of these investors have been kept in Fixed Deposit accounts with banks as per SEBI Regulations.

Investor Services

During the year, the fund put its best foot forward in terms of redressal of investor grievances addressing each and every individual investor complaint.

Change in Custodians

ABN Amro Bank who was the custodian for the schemes viz. Discovery Stock Fund, Bonanza Exclusive Growth Scheme Open, Libra Tax Shield, Libra Bond Fund, Libra Gilt Fund scheme had sold their custody and clearing business to Citibank in December 2004. Since Citibank is the custodian of the Starshare scheme, therefore, Citibank become the sole custodian for all the schemes managed by the Mutual Fund.

Future Outlook

First three months of FY 2005-2006 have witnessed one of the golden period for Indian Capital Market. During the period, BSE Sensex have crossed 7200 level, which is all time high. This record was possible on account of strong revival of foreign inflows and settlement of dispute in one of the largest corporate house in industry.

Now, the time has come when investment needs a very cautious approach and requires a re-look at the entire investment strategy not only by the individual investor but also by the Mutual Funds in general. The sensex may be quite volatile, as many technical analysts believe that index can soar close to the magical 5-digit level by 2007. Their presumption is based on the robust GDP Growth, under exposure of retail investors, strong earnings momentum, reforms in the right direction coupled with more FDI inflows and political stability. In the recent past, Japanese Funds have also entered in the Indian market in the big way, which is now being followed by funds from Singapore. As such, Indian Capital market is no more dependent on the inflows of FIIs funds from US only.

Schemes	*Investor complaints*			
	Received in previous year	*Received during the year*	*Redressed during the year*	*Outstanding 31.03.2005*
Starshare	260	245	245	NIL
Discovery stock fund	93	95	95	NIL
Libra tax shield	2	1	1	NIL
Libra bond fund	1	NIL	NIL	NIL
Libra Gilt fund	1	NIL	NIL	NIL
BONANZA exclusive growth scheme-open	35	29	29	Nil
Total	392	370	370	Nil

In India, Mutual Fund, on account of various steps taken in the past, the performance of all the schemes has shown considerable improvement. Our endeavor is not only to maintain this lead but also to increase the assets under management.

POLLUTION CONTROL

Essential requirements of all life and particularly mankind are land, water and air.

Our forefathers had robust health and long life due to hills with vegetation, sholas, perennial rivers, medicinal herbs, unpolluted water, tall hefty trees, pure air etc.

We are able to see now degradation all around and land, water, air getting polluted. We have advanced very much scientifically, much at the expense of nature. We have not cared the in-roads it made in nature in polluting the atmosphere. The environment is spoiled resulting in adverse effects. Acid rains started all over. Rivers, seas and water sources are poisoned by factory residues. The residues of automatic energy started threatening all kinds of life. Air is polluted at alarming rates. Unless counter measures are initiated to maintain nature and surroundings, all our scientific advancements will be null and void.

So our motto should be to protect the surroundings environment and nature.

Land Pollution

Large tracts of forest areas are getting denuded and destroyed altogether. It is estimated that in a year all over the globe one-lakh acres of forest area getting destroyed and taken out of forest sector. These lands turn into house sites etc., result in low rainfall. Land slides and erosion happens. Dams put-up at huge costs getting silted up and soil loose its fertility and altogether destroyed becoming inhospitable for cultivation.

Use of chemicals and synthetic fertilizers and reekless use of insecticides and pesticides altogether change the fertility of soil. Due to this, lot of decease's spread due to consuming eatables from these sort of bereft soils.

For making paper etc., lot of vegetation is destroyed. For making synthetic silk too lot of vegetation is destroyed.

Mining Activities

Cement factories, bauxite, and coal. mines involve destruction of large tracts of land that are thrown out of friendly atmosphere and bare ghastly appearance. Stone quarries are yet other such activity. It is estimated that many thousands of fauna and flora vanished from the earth due to our unfriendly activities resulting in upsetting balance of nature.

Water Pollution

Because of deforestation soon after rains there are floods. Water doesn't soak in due to run-off and poor see page. The rivers arising out of these mountains are not perennial. So water table is very low. This tells upon agriculture. Sub soil water also indiscriminately used resulting in water sources drying up.

Sub soil water also almost coming to an end. It is quite common to tap water illegally mostly on the banks of the rivers. Factories discharge their gutter water in to the rivers. So is the case with leather factories, paper factories, tapioca factories, distilleries etc.,

Gutter water of cities, towns mix in the rivers, lakes, wells and seas. The result is this water sources become unfit for drinking. Even fish etc, do not thrive. Estuary is a typical example of this. At huge cost Govt. of India is executing a project called purification of "Ganges River". Our ancient culture started flourishing and established mostly on the banks of the rivers. Even trade etc., flourished on the banks of rivers only. In our country rivers are held very sacred.

What is the Position to-day?

Poompukar our ancient cultural center on the banks of river cauvery has gone into ruins. Sand quarrying is another perilous activity happening recently. It is common to see animals {cattle} take bath on one side and man on the other side in the same water source. The same water is also taken for drinking.

Air Pollution

To get fresh air people throng beaches. Smoke is inimical to health. Smoke from motor vehicles, coal furnaces, thermal stations, atomic energy stations causing ill-health to humanity. The dust, ash and radiation from the above also contribute in ruining health. By smoking the polluted air, we get asthma and T'B. The TajMahal one of the Seven Wonders of the World is now threatened to become "Block TajMahal" due to the smoke coming out from a refinery at Mathura. Air is getting polluted by cement factories, leather factories, paper industries, sugar industries, dyeing factories and garment factories. No plants can grow in the normal way around these.

Ozone

This air layer prevents harmful rays of sun from directly hitting earth, thus protecting life on earth. It is feared unless pollution control measures are adopted, this ozone layer will get thinned and may even break {it has already broken at some places}. If this thinning and puncturing of ozone goes on unchecked the results will be:

(a) The global warming will go up which will result in the snow getting melted. This will raise the see level to 4 to 5 feet, submerging the coastal areas. We may be losing Rameswaram altogether. Bangladesh may sink. Japan may not be there.

(b) The harmful rays may wipe out all living beings on earth. we may develop skin eruptions, heart attacks etc.,

If this unpolluted air, noise, dust continues, we may lose our hearing capacity. Thus, deaf will be common.

Remedial Measures

We should not spit at will anywhere and every where. Remedial measures thus should start from this. Urination should not be done at any place. The habit of using dustbins must become our habit we should grow more trees and preserve the existing ones. It is estimated that a tree in its lifetime gives 17lakhs rupees worth benefit to mankind.

We must preserve wild life. We must create green belts along roads, railways, water channels, canals, air-port, factories etc., By these pollution is reduced, noise also getting reduced. Practice only "Contour cultivation". We should have "Eco-housing" programmes. We must go in for "River training programmes". Poisonous materials and residues should not be allowed to mix with water sources. Inflammable materials, explosives, acids etc., should be carefully planned while storing, transports etc.,

Workers should be given training. Factory residues should be purified. There are so many methods to purify poisonous materials. We must filter tanks etc., before letting it for consumption.

Factories should not be put up at all places. There should be enough thinking before establishing them as to then, where and how. Now there is control over establishing factories like there should be forest department clearance etc.

The cost of such NOC must be ensured and necessary staff should be recruited. Even for buying motor vehicles, "Green Car" system should be brought in.

Pollution Control Boards have been set up and Environment and Pollution Ministries have come up. There are rules to enforce this. Example,

(a) 1974 Water Pollution Control Act,

(b) 1981 Air Pollution Control Act,

(c) 1986 Environment Pollution Control Act.

Any one can report to Pollution Control Board officials on any factory not following the above rules. Any one can file cases in the court.

During 1993, 180 countries met at "Reo-de Genero" and discussed ways and means of pollution control and common programme has been divised universally We can go on writing like this in innumerable pages. All of us have a right to avail good air, water and good environment and to sustain good health. We should not be deprived of our rights.

RAILWAY PIONEERING INSTITUTE

Industry Profile

The first proposal for the construction of Railways in India were presented in 1844 to the East India Company headed by R.M. Stephenson, who later became agent and managing director of East India Railways which was one of the first two Railway Companies that found floor tool in India. The other was the great Indian peninsula Railway Company.

On 16th of April 2003 Indian Railways entered in to yet another era, having crossed 150 Glorious years of dedicated service to the nation, and can rightly feel a sense of pride, achievement and satisfaction. The Railways served as the infrastructural framework around which the country's economy was built providing transport linkage, at a time when other sectors of transport were virtually in the nascent stage. The railways are really at threshold and looking inward and trying to understand what went wrong in between and what has to be done to help Indian Railways re arrange as strong and vibrant organization. Thus ICF came in to planning of construction.

Role of ICF in Indian Railways

ICF is one the biggest production units in Indian Railways. The main function of the production unit is the production of coaches to meet the requirement of Indian Railways as well as coaches for export to foreign countries. The coaches produced by ICF were exported to countries like Taiwan, Zimbabwe, Bangladesh and Malaysia and thus have earned foreign exchange also. ICF has developed over 100 designs of coaches to suit the varied requirements of Indian Railways and for export. Apart from manufacture of coaches ICF also supplies some of the essential components as spares to Indian Railways.

Rise of ICF

ICF, the premier rail coach manufacturing facility was launched in October 2nd 1955, which is located at Perambur, Chennai. This is one of the major production unit owned by Indian Government and governed by ministry of Railways. This is also biggest rail coach production unit in Asia and fourth-largest type in world. Since the commencement of factory, many types of coaches were manufactured and these run all over the world. It has an area of 19,22,500 sq.m. With a capital, amounting to Rs. 125 crores. The Integral Coach Factory is a production unit of the Indian Railways, which was setup under the first five-year plans. The ICF coachbuilders built in collaboration with M/s. Swiss car elevators and Manufacturing Corporation of Switzerland. Sri Jawaharlal Nehru called it a "modern temple of India". With more than 100 employees at the starting level and at present there are around 14,000 employees on the role. The success is not only because of technological transfer and design but also the motivational aspect given by the frontline management from the grass root level of employee, taking care of their welfare aspects, irrespective of their level of stress.

Because of teamwork of the employees this has been achieved. In the year 1985 a similar coach factory was inaugurated at Kapurtala near Punjab with 5000 employees calling it as "Rail Coach Factory".

Golden Jubliee

Integral Coach Factory (ICF), Perambur, the country's largest railway coach manufacturing unit, is celebrating its golden jubilee. Established in 1955 with Swiss collaboration to build integral passenger coaches of all welded steel design, ICF has come a long way. ICF has so far manufactured and supplied around 35,784 coaches making, the factory the largest producer of coaches in Asia. It now manufactures coaches of 250 different designs for three different gauges, and with increased speed potential, with a turnover of Rs. 747 crores in 2004. Railway Board had asked ICF to increase production to 1,250 coaches from the current capacity of 1,100 per year.

Modern machines were acquired from a broad and works are onto build a new plant for automation of painting of coaches. By year-end, the new paint shop would enable automatic spray painting. Production is getting gradually modernized in term of use of materials. The progress has been from ordinary steel to corten steel (copper-bearing corrosion-resistant steel) and some parts of fittings like brake fittings are now made of stainless steel. A full-fledged research and development wing is currently operational at the factory where engineers develop coaches with safety and travel comfort for passengers in mind. Besides, sharp edges in interior fixtures were rounded off and upholstery works improved to impart a more aesthetic look. Redesigning of coaches, aerodynamic front-end Diesel. Electric Multiple Units, Luxury Coaches for Deccan Odyssey and other were done using indigenous technology.

A few passenger-friendly amenities developed and incorporated in ICF-manufactured coaches for long-distance trains include: emergency exit windows on both sides of second-class sleeper and AC coaches, exit latches on roof and floor, use of fire-retardant material and paints.

The factory has also manufactured luxury trains for different tourism departments like Royal Orient Express for

Gujarat Tourism Corporation, Palace-on-wheels for Rajasthan Tourism Development Corporation and Deccan Odyssey for Maharastra Tourism Development Corporation. ICF has made a mask in the export arena against competition from advanced countries and has exported 359 bogies and 452 coaches to Thailand, Myanmar, Taiwan, Zambia, Philippines, etc.

The Fifty Years of ICF

- 1948-N Gopalasamy Aiyengar, Minister of Transport and Railways decided to set up factory in Perambur for producing coaches.
- 1951-Site Investigation and Planning started at Perambur.
- 1953-Technical aid agreement with Swiss car & elevator manufacturing corporation Ltd.
- 1954-Technical Training School inaugurated to train craftsmen for factory.
- 1955-ICF inaugurated by Prime Minister Jawaharlal Nehru on Oct. 2nd.
- 1956 -First Indigenous Coach launched by President of India Rajendra Prasad.
- 1961-Furnishing Factory was opened and finished coach was flagged off.
- 1968-Coaches for Rajdhani Super Fast Trains launched.
- 1977-Second-class Sleeper Coaches with cushier berth were launched.
- 1989-90-Shatabdi Coaches with speed capacity of 160.kmph were launched.
- 1990-Modernisation and Production augmentation to 1,000 coaches year was achieved.
- 1991-92-Palace on wheels for Rajasthan Tourism Development Corporation was built.

- 1993-94-700HP Diesels Electric Multiple Units (DEMU) was produced.
- 1999-2000-DEMU of 1400 hp was launched.
- 2004-DEMUs with aerodynamic profile were launched.
- 2004-Modern Coaches for Janshatabdi, Deccan Odyssey Luxury Train and new generation EMUs were built.

The ICF, which is spread over area of 193.47 hectors of land, has two divisions.

1. *Shell Division:* Here the frame and body of the coach are developed.
2. *Furnishing Division:* Here seating, electrical work, painting, assembling etc are undertaken.

The two divisions are located about 2.5km apart and are connected by an exclusive rail unit for the movement of shell to furnishing.

For the purpose of technical, financial and cost control, the factory has been broadly divided into five major departments.

(a) Production shops
(b) Service shop inside the workshop
(c) Service shop outside the workshop
(d) Stores department
(e) General department

Production Capacity

The factory has production capacity of producing more than 1100 coaches with the existing infrastructure. In 2000-2001, the number of coaches produced was 1057; the target fixed for the year 2001-2002 has been achieved with 1024 coaches. The productions of shell up to June 2004 were 36,048, average production per month comes around 60 coaches and in a year it comes around 1150 to 1200 coaches.

Types of Coaches Manufactured

The factory has produced many types of coaches for Indian Railways and foreign countries. Some types of coaches include:

- EMU motors
- EMU trailers
- A/C coaches
- Conventional coaches
- Self propelled coaches
- Special export coaches
- Motor coaches for electric multiple unit
- Diesel hydraulic multiple units
- Diesel electrical tower car
- Mainline EMU coaches

The factory has developed lightweight stainless steel body coaches as an innovation recently.

ISO 9001 and ISO 14001 Certification

The factory has been awarded the ISO 9001 asd ISO 14001 certification for quality, System covering the entire factory as well as the environment and all activities of design, development, manufacturing and commissioning of powered and non-powered a/c and non ac railway passenger coaches including luxury coaches. ISO 14001 on EMS mainly focus on enhanced internal management system efficiency, reduced waste, pollution prevention and improved environmental performance. The certificate has been awarded by the international reputed certifying agency RWTVY of Germany. ICF was the first among the Indian Railway Production Unit to get ISO 9001 and ISO 14001 certificates for the entire factory.

Suggestions

The ICF should start manufacturing coaches for bullet trains abroad by getting contracts. Slowly our railways too implement "bullet trains", in our country.

Such other modern things must be done here thus competing with any other country in the world.

All efforts should be made only to expand and proliferate the activities. Many concessions like land, electricity, water can be thought of. Under no circumstances there must be curtailment, which may lead to the unemployment etc.

SECRET OF SUCCESS

Introduction

We take immense pleasure in introducing the famous industrial Icon of our region Thirumigu K.M. Govindarajanar. He is 86 years old an idealist of Gandhiji and a renounced freedom fighter. He is a complete man in every aspects of Gudiyattam town. He is a successful industrialist, educationalist and social worker. He is a man of courage, hard work and integrity.

Having highly qualified and large heart he is the man to be admired as an icon of the rural town of Gudiyattam.

He served much of his life for the independence of our country.

He gave the best years of his life for the betterment of social, Educational and civilization progress of the town.

He constantly strives for the upliftment of the downtrodden society of this area.

Biography

Thirumigu K.M. Govindarajanar was born at Gudiyattam (Vellore district in a middle class family. His father Thirumigu K.M. ManikhaMudaliyar was a traditional moneylender and agriculturist. He had five sons and three daughters and K.M.G. was the eldest. He is a self-made man who moulded his personality even at a very early age.

His rich experience in dyeing cotton fabrics at the age of 20 induced him to start his own industry during 1960 the South Indian Mills Ltd. At Gudiyattam with an authorized capital of Rs. 5 lakhs and paid up capital of Rs. 3 lakhs.

His dedication and sincerity in the business made him to run his business successfully. As chairman and managing director are under his leadership the company involved in exports.

He sacrificed his life and soul for our national freedom." The very first national flag hoisted in Red Fort Delhi was the product of his company the South Indian Silks Ltd., Gudiyattam. This was the talk of the nation then it is a matter of pride to this self–made industrial icon of the rural town of Gudiyattam.

Achievements

The achievements of Thirumugu K.M.Govindarajanar cannot be expressed in few words or few pages. All his achievements briefly an in:

(a) Industrial

Thiru. K.M.G acquired major share in South Indian Ltd., and become the managing director, which was originally manufacturing silk fabrics started in exports. In future it will manufacture poly cotton and yarns.

He entered in the film industry under the banner Geetha pictures, Madhurai veeran, Mahadevi, Veerapandiya Kattabomman, Parasakthi, Kadhalukku Mariyadhai, Thenkasi etc., celebrated silver jubilee.

(b) Educational

His sole interest in education led him to start an elementary school at Gudiyattam at the age of 32.

Later he started Thiruvalluvar higher secondary schools, which has become a state level renounced school for its high standard of education. Total number of students studied in this school is above 7000/-.

In the millennium years 2000, he started K.M.G. College of arts and science. With a strength of 800 students now. Recently, he started Thiruvalluvar Teacher Training Institute.

(c) Social

Thiru K.M. Govindarajanar took active part in the endured freedom struggle and endured all the atrocities caused by the British rulers.

He was the Municipal chairman of Gudiyattam Municipality for 5 years. He did the spade–works for 9000 drinking water facility; bus stand for Gudiyattam; sanitation and maternity welfare.

He has immense love for Tamil and its culture. For the development of Tamil language, he recently started Muthamil Klakiya Mandram and it is doing well.

A president of various renovation committees for temples he constructed many temples and mended many dilapidated ones.

Nearly 300 poor students from in and around Gudiyattam are getting free education.

Secret of his Success

He inculcates a sense of collectivism among the workers and drives them to work as a team.

Workers problems are analyzed thread amicable and Solutions are arrived at bare are solved in with quality.

Efficacious remedial measures are invented infusing every one around him to work enthusiastically.

Future Plans

He proposed to open an orphanage in the name and style of K.M.G orphanage center to cater to the needs of orphans.

He proposed to start B.Sc, B.Ed., M.C.A; and MBA next acedamic year.

He proposed to construct an indoor stadium Gymnastic center, which Gudiyattam town is lacking.

Awards and Rewards

The "Kalvikho" "Kalvithanthai" "Samaya nallinakka kavalar" were conferred an him. He was honoured by the award 'for the sake of honour' by rotary club of Gudiyattam. Youth of Gudiyattam town recently him as honoured 'Manava nala chemmal'.

Conclusion

Herculean efforts and Himalayan achievements of Thiru K.M., Govindarajan. Enhanced the reputation of Gudiyattam. He is highly religious with a single motto of "Ondre Kulam oruvanne Devan". He himself finds happiness by saying "Maanavar Sirippil Eraivanai Kaangirean", Gudiyattam is blessed by the birth of this stalwart, towering personality and a great man.

SOCIO-ECONOMIC CONDITIONS OF TRIBALS IN JAVADHI HILLS OF VELLORE & TRIVANNAMALAI DISTRICTS

Profile

The Javadhi hills form part of the Eastern ghats lying in Vellore & Tiruvannamalai District of Tamil Nadu in north latitude 11^0-59^0 to 13^0 –15^0 and west longitude 78^0 –10^0 to 78^0 –50^0. These hills rise steeply from the plains forming an undulating plateau on the top of about 500 to 800 metres elevation. These mountain ranges runs in the South-west to North-east direction to a length of about 100 kms and width varying from 25 to 40 kms enclosing small valleys. The outer slopes are rocky, steep and precipitous.

Drainage

The entire Javadhis comes under the catchment of Palar river. The Cheyyar, Amirdhi Ar, Padavettar and Pambar are the main tributaries of Palar that have their catchments in Javadhis. They are all semiperennial.

Climate

The climate of Javadhis is always milder and more pleasant than the plains. The maximum temperature is in the month of May (44^0 c.) and minimum is in the month of January (11^0 C). Generally it receives both South-West and North-East Monsoons. The average rainfall is about 900 m.m.

Forests

Javadhis supports one of the largest and most valuable block of forests containing climax vegetation of varied species including Sandal. Bamboo and a variety of Minor Forest Produce yielding trees. The following are the general forest types met with.

1. Southern dry mixed deciduous Forest (5A/C3).
2. Southern dry deciduous scrub forests (5A/DE1).
3. Southern dry tropical riverrain forests (5A/IS1).
4. Tropical dry evergreen forests–Carnatic evergreen forests (7/C1).
5. Tropical dry evergreen forests (Hill evergreen forests).
6. Tropical dry semi-evergreen forests.

The Javadhis forms the home of Sandalwood, which yields the bulk of forest revenue in Tamil Nadu state.

People

The principal inhabitants of Javadhis are Scheduled Tribes called Malayalis. There is no record of their origin. There is a belief that these Malayalis originally belonged to Kancheepuram belonging to a community of cultivators and that they took refuge in these hills when Tippusultan started his southern conquests. They are Hindus by religion and preserved a set of customs all their own. Their staple food consists of Cholam, Ragi, Varagu or Samai supplemented by some vegetable preparation. They rear cows, sheeps, pigs, buffaloes and fowls. They are not as hard working as the plains people and their cultivation is not intensive. They live in low roofed mud huts. Each hamlet has an oorgounden or Nattan as their leader.

The extent of Javadhis is about 3060 Sq. kms. of which the land area occupied by the tribals will be 307 Sq. kms. The total population is 61327 of which 38,706 are tribals constituting 63,1% of total population.

The tribals of Javadhis and forests of are ecologically and economically inseparable. They have co-existed since time immemorial and will continue to live in the most symbiotic manner to the benefit of both. In Javadhis the agriculture and animal husbandary farms the dominant economic activities and they are dependant on forests to a large extent. Agricultural implements and tools are made from wooden poles and bamboos. The maintenance of cattle for agriculture purpose depends to a great extent on the existence of grazing facility. Animal husbandary and diary development programmes are related to the availability of grass fodder, leaves etc. house construction in tribal areas is undertaken with materials collected from forests. Timber. Bamboo and grass are used in house construction.

The tribals form part and parcel of forest ecosystem. The tribal economy and forest development are interdependent and therefore the following programmes have been undertaken by the Forest Department.

1. At the time of revenue settlement al Javadhi hill tribes were given land for cultivation.
2. The tribals are permitted to graze their cattle inside the forests freely.
3. They are allowed to cut and remove grass and fodder for their cattle.
4. They are permitted to remove thatch grass and small timber for agricultural and house construction purposes.
5. The Tribals are provided occupation in the form of extraction of sandalwood, formation and maintenance of roads, afforestation works, and collection of minor forest produce. Annually about 25 to 30 thousand dead sandalwood trees are extracted and carried to roadside depots by tribals. About 2 lakhs of rupees are disbursed annually as wages to tribals creating 25,000 mandays of employment. In the afforestation work about 5 lakh

rupees are spent and about 62,500 mandays of employment generated. About 300 tending mazdoor are employed throughout year for protection and tending of sandalwood trees creating about 1,09,500 mandays of employment annually.

Education

There are one Higher Secondary School, one High School and sixteen elementary Schools for the tribals run by Forest Department in Javadhis. The details of schools run by Forest Department are as follows:

Name of School	Students (Number)
1. Higher Secondary School, Jamnamarathur	557
2. High School, Pudurnadu	313
3. Elementary Schools (Total 16 number)	2382

All the students are provided free text books and uniforms annually. The Chief Ministers Nutritious Noon-Meal Scheme is being implemented by the Forest Department in all the Schools. The hill tribes are mainly the organizers of the noon-meal scheme and about thirty four persons are employed for this purpose. The children's are provided with free hostel facilities at Jamnamarathur. The special feature of the Higher Secondary School art Jamnamarathur is that it has the best archery team consisting of tribal boys and girls. It has won various All India tournaments from 1980 onwards. There are about 35 teachers employed in the above school and most of them have been provided with residential quarters. The tribal schools have produced many men of recognition in Government and private sectors. Recently a Swimming pool and Indoor Auditorium were constructed and added on to the facilities available at the Jamnamarathur Higher Secondary School.

Approach Roads

The total length of roads and bridal paths in Javadhis is more than 400 kms. The forest Department is maintaining and improving the above roads. It provides the facility of surfaces transportation for tribals in addition to providing employment to a larger number of them. There are about 71 Mazdoors employed throughout the year for the maintenance of the above roads.

Lamp Co-operative Society

A large area multipurpose co-operative society is functioning at Jamnamarathur for the benefit of the tribals. Minor Forest Produces lease are allotted to the Society at a concessional of minor forest produce like gallnut and tamarind. In 1987-88 M.F.P lease units worth about 3 lakhs have been allotted to LAMP co-operative Society at Jamnamarathur.

Drinking Water

Protected water supply from 25 draw wells dug and maintained by Forest Department are continued for the benefit of tribals of Javadhis. Four overhead tanks with electric pumps are being maintained for the benefit of too largely populated villages namely Jamnamarathur, Amirdhi, Kuttathur and Pallankottai. Schemes are being implemented to extend the same facilities to other villages.

Sandal Estate

SCHEME UNDER I.T.D.P.–Integrated Tribal
Development Programme–Forestry Sector
Under Tribal Sub–Plan.

From 1986-87 Sandal Estate is under implementation in Vellore Circle with a view to improve the sandal growing stock and to provide employment opportunities to tribals. Simultaneously the living conditions of the tribals will also be improved by providing drinking water facilities, approach roads, provision of apiary boxes and training in apiary, planting of local trees etc. As per this scheme, about 16 lakhs of rupees have already been spent in 1986-87 and another about 16 lakhs will be spent in 1987-88.

The following seven villages have been selected as Programme villages and 7000 ha. of Sandal Forests were set apart for the scheme.

1. Melkomutteri
2. Komutteri
3. Kanaganeri
4. Vellikottai
5. Kunikanthur
6. Palankotteri
7. Kottathur

In these Villages 271 families are benefited under this Scheme. Details of works, and mandays generated and benefits are given in the Appendix.

Sandal Estate Scheme

Component	*Amount Spent Rs.*	*No.of Families Benefited*	*Mandays Generated*	*Remarks*
1	2	3	4	5
1. Sandal Tending operation (Enumeration, climber cutting etc.,).	90273-00		11280	
2. Improvement of growing stock.	98950-00		10 000	
3. Soil and Moisture Conservation works (Construction of checkdams and percolation ponds in R.F. adjoining to villages).	201830-00		20000	
4. Creation of Nuclear sandal plot.	251380-00		9050	
5. Central permanent nursery	95430-00		5500	
6. Creation of Bee pasture	22000-00	20 Families		
7. Extraction of rough cleaning of sandal wood	132000-00		16500	
B. Other Welfare works	Rs.			
(i) Repairs to old well 2 Nos.	6240-00		750	
(ii) Construction of overhead tank-3 Nos.	182885-00		13000	
(iii) Repairs to Cattle pond–2 Nos	42635-00		3730	
(iv) Improving approach road-3 roads for 3 Villages	120430-00		13000	
(v) Construction of Labour Shed	40622-00		3000	

Enefits Extended to the Hill Tribes of Javadhis

Sl. No.	Name of the Scheme	No. of persons directly benefited annually (approximate)	No.of mandays (approximate)	Money spent	Remarks
1.	Sandalwood extraction	95	75000	600000/-	
2.	Afforestation works	700	68750	566115/-	
3.	Sandalwood Tending	120	75000	980640/-	
4.	Road workers	120	38000	303995/-	
5.	Construction of new roads and bridges	50	16100	129565/-	
6.	Building works	150	22250	356624/-	
7.	Collection of Tamarind/ Gallnut etc.,	200	37500	300000/-	
8.	Noon Meal Scheme employees	34	12410	24480/-	
9.	Hostel facilities in Forest High School	280	—	238000/-	

Other Beneeits

Name of the Scheme	Indirect benefits value of the concession given	No. of persons benefited	Remarks
Free grazing and fodder	77560-00	———	Cows and – 29972 Buffaloes Sheep, Goats and-17616 Pigs
Thatching materials and small timber for house construction	990000-00	3300 families or 13200 persons annually.	Generally houses are re-constructed once in three years.
School facilities	929000-00	3252 Students	One Higher Secondary School-One High School 16 Elementary School 2 Hostels
Fire rewards Provision of protected water	3000-00	4 Villages	A nominal sum in appreciation of their work of assisting the Forest officials.

THE POWER OF WOMEN AND THEIR ACHIEVEMENTS IN WOMEN ENTREPRENEURSHIP

Introduction

In earlier days women were confined to the four walls of houses and led a protected life. In the present modern society they have come out of the walls and take part in all sorts of activities competing successfully equal to men. This has become possible because of the safeguards, industrialization and urbanization. It has been proved globally that women have been performing exceedingly well in various fields such as education, administration, politics, sports, medicine, aeronautics, trade and industries, social work, transports, science and technology etc. The very fact that the world's largest democracy [India] was headed by a woman Smt. Indira Gandhi is a big complement to the capacity, caliber and character of women. Thus Women Entrepreneurs are helpful to the society in various departments to economic and social development of our country.

Concept of Women Entrepreneurs

A women or a group of women who initiate, organize and run a business enterprise is defined as women entrepreneur[s]. The Government of India has defined women entrepreneur as "an enterprise owned and controlled by a women having a minimum financial interest of 51% of the capital and giving at least 51% of the employment generated in the enterprise to women".

Women entrepreneurs are those women who conceive the idea of a business enterprise, initiate it, organize and combine the factors of production, operate the enterprise, undertake risks and manage the economic uncertainty involved in running a business enterprise.

Power of Women

The social –economic advancement of a country can best be judged by the status and position, which it can bestow on its women. One of the most important changes that have taken place in recent times is the growing status of women. Economic factors among others have freed women from the shackles of outworn tradition, prejudice and ignorance. The world of work is undergoing a transformation. Although women are assuming new roles at all levels, women moving into the middle and upper echelons of management are destined to exert considerable influence on the future of business large have already made dramatic progress in selecting, developing and retaining women executives, especially during the last 20 years. Despite barriers and obstacles, some women do make it to the top. They exhibit the technical domain in which qualities needed for excellence are generally considered feminine viz., warmth, patience, hard work, sincerity, understanding and sensitivity. They enter the arena where expectations about leadership and management are more compatible with the male stereotype and masculine traits such as forcefulness, decisiveness, risk-taking, problem analysis, negotiating and bargaining. In recent years women in larger numbers are entering the managerial world. it was the last bastion of male dominance. Women have already entered and made themselves acceptable in infrastructral services such as technicians, doctors, engineers and pilots. Entry into the managerial cadre is a reality but a difficult process. Many aspiring women have found the doors of the organizations to similarly employ men and deny the opportunity to similarly educated skilled and trained women. One woman management graduate literally gate crashed the interview and demanded that she be tested on interview and demanded that she be tested on managerial skill, knowledge, attitude and her capabilities. She broke the barriers and got the job.

Functions of Women Entrepreneurs

Similarly to men entrepreneurs women entrepreneurs have to perform all the functions involved in setting up an enterprise such as idea generation and scanning, determination of objectives, project preparation, product analysis, determination of forms of business organization, combination of factors of production etc.

Fredrick Harbinson has listed out the following five functions of a women entrepreneur.

1. Exploration of the prospects of starting a new business enterprise.
2. Undertaking of risks and the handling of economic uncertainties involved in business.
3. Introduction of innovations or imitation of innovations.
4. Coordination, administration and control.
5. Supervision and leadership.

The major entrepreneurial functions can be broadly classified under three categories.

1. Risk bearing,
2. Organization,
3. Innovations.

Profile of Women Entrepreneurs

Woman entrepreneur may be described as a woman of commitment who is independently employed and has a close relationship with her father. After obtaining a graduate degree, she gets married. She enters into the fields of entrepreneurial venture at the age of late 30's or early 40's when her children are somewhat self-sufficient. She is usually from a middle class family and her biggest problem is lack of sufficient business training especially in the financial area. However in the recent years, with increase in literacy level the women have gained confidence to do all the work, which was hitherto considered as the prerogative of men. They have shown excellent results and proved that no field is unapproachable to trained and determined modern women.

Qualities of a Woman Entrepreneur

Some of the outstanding qualities of a woman entrepreneur are given below:

Accepts challenges, Adventurous, Ambitious, Conscientious, Full of drive, Educated, Enthusiastic, Determined to excel, Hardworking, Keen to learn and imbibe new ideas, Patient, Experienced, Industrious, Intelligent, Motivated, Perseverance, Skilful, studious, Optimistic.

Psycho-social Barriers

Though some women entrepreneurs are performing exceedingly well in various fields of activities, the fear of success haunt women in general. Growth of entrepreneurship is impeded by various psycho- social factors. Some of them are given below.

1. Poor self image of women
2. Inadequate motivation
3. Discriminating treatment
4. Faulty socialization
5. Role conflict
6. Lack of courage and self-confidence

7. Cultural values
8. Inadequate encouragement
9. Lack of social acceptance
10. Unjust social, economic and cultural system
11. Lack of freedom of expression
12. Afraid of failures of criticism
13. Susceptible to negative attitudes
14. Non-persistent attitudes
15. Low dignity of labour
16. Lacking in leadership qualities such as planning, organizing, controlling, coordinating and directing.

Growth and Development of Women Entrepreneurship

The US Bureau of census reported in 1977 that there were only, 7,02,000 business that were owned by women. This was only 7.1% of the total business firms in us. However, the number is increasing at a rapid rate. In 1984, according to the Internal Revenue Service, the number of female sole proprietorship was 3.1 million or 22% of all sole proprietorships. The highest number of women is found in laundries, dry cleaning, hair- dressing, private nurseries, hotels etc. In US, the Small Business Administration [SBA], a Government controlled agency provides financial assistance and offers courses in counseling to improve managerial competence among women entrepreneurs.

In India, women are regarded as the "better half of the society". In reality our society is still male dominating one. Due to our traditional socio-cultural conventions and taboos, the development of women entrepreneurship is very low in our country. In earlier days women were engaged in the unorganized sectors like agriculture, handicrafts, handlooms and cottage based industries. The entry of Indian into entrepreneurship is a recent phenomenon.

In the beginning women entrepreneurship was identified as an extension of kitchen activities and denoted by *3ps* namely *pickles, powder and pappad.* The increase in literacy level and awareness about trade and industries motivated the women to shift from *3ps to 3ES* namely *Engineering, Electronics and Energy.*

Indian woman gets into the business due to two reasons namely *"pull factors"* and *"push factors"*. Pull factors encourage women to have an independent occupation. These factors influence the women entrepreneurs to choose a profession as a challenge and as an adventure with an urge to do something new. Push factors are those, which compel women to take up business enterprises to get over financial difficulties and responsibility is thrust on them due to unfortunate family circumstances.

Tenth Five Year Plan 2002-2007

During the 10th five year plan, women entrepreneurship are considered as special importance to the economic development of our country due to the following reasons.

1. To treat women as specific target groups in all development programmes.
2. To devise and diversify vocational training facilities for women to suit their varied needs and skills.
3. To provide assistance for marketing of products of women entrepreneurs.
4. To involve women in decision-making process.

In India several institutional arrangement have been made to develop women entrepreneurship. The commercial banks and state financial corporations provide loans to women entrepreneurs on preferential basis and concessional terms. SIDCO and DICs provide loans, subsidies and grants to small-scale women entrepreneurs in preparing project reports, purchasing machinery, training the staff etc.

To develop women entrepreneurship the United Nations declared the decade 1975-85 as the decade foe women. The UNIDO preparatory meeting on the *Role of Woman in Industrialization in Developing Countries held at Vienna in February, 1978, identified* several constraints such as social attitudes, institutional barriers, inadequate employment opportunities, inappropriate and inadequate training, insufficient information and so on which held women back from participating in industrial activities. The world conference of the United Nations Decade for Women held at Denmark in 1980 adopted a programme for promoting women entrepreneurship.

The first National Conference of Women Entrepreneurs held at New Delhi in 1981. Recommended the need for development of the country. It also called for priority to women in allotment of land, sheds, sanction of power, licensing, financial assistance etc. national alliance to young entrepreneurs [NAYE] had setup a women's wing in 1975. Three international conferences and 8 Nationals conventions of women entrepreneurs have been organized by NAYE in different cities of India.

In 1989, the industrial development bank of India [IDBI] setup the Mahila Udayam Nidhi [MUN] and Mahila Vikas Nidhi [MVN] schemes to help women entrepreneurs. The MUN had provided 15% equity assistance for new units with project cost not exceeding Rs.10 lakhs. The MUN scheme extends aid to voluntary agencies in decentralized industries for training-cum-production centers and management and skill up gradation. The industrial policy Resolution of 1991 emphasized the need for conducting special entrepreneur-ship development programmes for women. This policy also recommended product and process oriented courses enabling women to start small-scale industries.

The seminar on "Women and Rural Entrepreneurship" held at Madurai Kamaraj University, in 1990 arrived at the following two conclusions and recommendations.

1. Women are not weak but very strong
2. The industrial and business opportunities are many electronics, engineering, plastic injection, moulding, food and allied activities, pharmaceuticals, energy etc.

Centre for entrepreneurship development [CED] at Madurai, is conducting entrepreneurship training programme for women at reputed educational institutions under the sponsorship of SIDBI. The CED has recently taken up a project sponsored by the International Labour Organization [ILO] to provide entrepreneurship training to 2400 mothers of child labourers at Tirupur and Virudhunagar.

Recently, in Tamilnadu, the government had initiated to set up a women's industrial park called 'Tirumullaivoyal Women's Industrial Park' at Ambathur near Chennai. The park is proposed to setup in an area of 218 acres of land. The development plots and industries sheds will be allotted to women entrepreneurs through SIDCO.

In Tamilnadu, entrepreneurship training was given to one-lakh women in 2001-2002 and it has been proposed to give training to 1.25 lakh women during the year 2002-03.

The growth of women's education increases their participation in the non-agriculture professions. Women are gradually coming forward to face challenges and assume responsibilities in various fields-economic-social- and political.

The number of women entrepreneurs in the field of engineering and electronic is on the rise. Women entrepreneurs manufacturing solar cookers in Gujarat, small foundries in Maharashtra and T.V. capacitors in Orissa have proved beyond doubt that given the opportunities, they can excel their male counterparts.

Case studies of several women entrepreneurs have revealed their women possess a futuristic outlook and the capacity to nurture new enterprises. These case studies highlight the problems faced by women entrepreneurs and steps taken by women entrepreneurs to overcome the various obstacles to succeed in their ventures the active participation of women entrepreneurs is essential in the development of small-scale industry.

Problems of Women Entrepreneurs

The basic problem of woman entrepreneur is being a woman. In many developing countries marriage is treated as the only carrier for women. Despite the constitutional and legal equality, women suffer from male reservations. This attitude of reservations creates problems at all levels like family support, training, licensing, banking and marketing. Some of the specific problems encountered by women entrepreneurs are listed below.

Problem of Finance

Finance is the "life-blood" for any enterprise. The access of women to external sources of funds is limited for the reason that they do not generally own properties on their name. Financial institutions consider women less credit worthy and discourage women borrowers on the belief that they may leave their business at any time. Under these circumstances the women entrepreneurs are found to rely on their own savings and loans from friends and relatives, which may not be adequate.

Scarcity of Raw Material

Most of the women enterprises are suffering from the scarcity of raw materials and inputs besides their high cost. In the purchase of raw material, the middle- men either denies discount or give the minium discount to the women entrepreneurs.

Stiff Competition

Women entrepreneurs do not have organizational set up and they are not able to spend much money for canvassing and advertisement. They have to face a stiff competition from both organized sector and male entrepreneurs marketing their products.

Limited Mobility

The mobility of women in India is highly limited due to humiliating attitude of men towards them.

Familities

The main duty of Indian women is to look after the members of their family. This leaves little time and energy to devote to business.

Lack of Education

In India more than 50% of the women are still illiterate. Lack of qualitiative education leads to unawareness of business technology and market knowledge and causes low achievement motivation. It also creates problems for women in setting up and running of business.

Male Dominated Society

Though the constitution of India speaks of equality between sexes, in practice women are treated next to men. This male domination serves as an impedient to the entry of women into business.

Low Risk Bearing Ability

Risk bearing is an essential requisite of successful entrepreneur. Most of the Indian women are less educated and economically not independent. This reduces their ability to bear risk involved in running a business.

Besides the above problems there are some other problems, which are comman to both male and female entrepreneurs. They are inadequate infrastructural facilities, shortage of power, high cost of production, social attitude, low need for achievement and socio economic constraints.

Suggestions for the Development of Women Entrepreneurs:

Today there is a greater awareness among women. Educating women is absolutely essential in straightening their personality. The need of the hour is to provide an opportunity in a conducive atmosphere, free from gender differences. Today no field is unapproachable to trained and determined modern women. To make the movement of women entrepreneurship a success, both the government and non-Government agencies have to play a vital role on the following lines.

- Priorities in allotment of industrial estates to women entrepreneurs.
- Adequate training programmes to women including mobile training centers.
- Financial assistance at subsidized interest rate.
- Assistance in marketing of their products by giving preference to their products in Government's purchasing policy.
- A majority of women entrepreneurs are from middle class families with low technical education, but desire to become entrepreneurs. Their potential should be identified and trained.
- One single nodal agency may be established to provide adequate infrastructural facilities such as flow of adequate working capital, technology, electricity, land and marketing facilities.

Women Entrepreneurship in India

In India, marriage is the only career for most women. Even professionly, they have confined their activities to teaching, office work, nursing and medicine. It is rarely that they enter professions like enginnering and business. In 1990, the Indian female population was 437.10 million representing 46.5 percent of the total population. There are 126.48 million women workforce, out of which only 1,85,900 women were self employed. Majority of them are engaged in the unorganized sectors like agriculture, agro based industries. There were 295680 women entrepreneurs of the total 2.64 million entrepreneurs in India during 1995-96. Of this, a majority were concentrated in low paid, low skilled, low technology and low productivity jobs in the rural and unorganized sector. The new industrial policy has stressed the importance of entrepreneurship among women. This would help improve their economic and social conditions. This would help improve their economic and social conditions. This policy has redefined women's units' as units in which they have the majority share holdings and management control.

In 1996, the department of small-scale industry under the ministry of industry had taken the initiative to train one lakh women entrepreneurs to take up trade related activities.

Women Entrepreneurs in Several Industries

Today we see women entrepreneurs in several industries namely electronics, enginnering, readymade garments, eatables, handicrafts, doll making, poultry, plastics, soap, ceramics, printing, nurseries, crèches, drugs, textile designing, dairy, canning, knitting, beauty parlours, jewellery design, solar cooker etc. some other potential areas are bio-technology, information technology, tourism and other service sectors.

"Women entrepreneurs-An exploratory study of Hyderabad" reveals that the motivational factors of self interest and inspiration from others are critical factors that lead one towards successful woman entrepreneur. The challenge and adventure to do something new, liking for business and independent occupation are some of the attractive leverages for women.

Successful Women Entrepreneurs

A selected representatives of successful women entrepreneurs are mentioned here.

Smt. Sumati Moraji-Shipping Corporation

Smt. Sharayu Daftary–Automobile Radiators

Smt. Chandragandhi Govindarajulu–Chandra Textiles, Coimbatore.

Smt. Radha Thiyagarajan–Thiyagarajar Mills, Madurai.

Smt. Ragashree Pathy–Rajashree Group of Companies, Coimbatore.

Smt. Malliga Seenivasan–Tractor and Farm Equipments.

Smt. D. Jayalakshmi Devaraj

Managing Director, Sri Vigneswara Group of Companies, Coimbatore.

Smt. D. Jayalakshmi Devaraj was just like any other housewife till june 1983. After the sudden demise of her husband, she took up the challenge of running the industry started by her husband. The total sales of the industry has been raised from 33 lakhs in 1984 to Rs.50 lakhs in 1988. She was the winner of the CODDISSIA award 1989 for the best women entrepreneur.

Smt. Rajashree Pathy

Chairperson and Managing Director of Raja Shree Group of Companies, Coimbatore.

In 1990, Ms. Rajashree pathy took on the mantle of the company when her father died. Under her able leaders the Rajashree group has grown to a turn over of Rs.300 crores from 50 crores in 1990. The group has expanded by setting up two new units each in the sugar and textile field apart from automobile retailing business.

To upgrade her skills ms.pathy underwent a "owner/ president management programme" at Harvard Business School between 1994–96. She was also selected as one of the members of global leadership for tomorrow Davos, Switzerland. The hallmark of Ms. Pathy's legacy has been optimal utilization of existing facilities and cashing in diversification opportunities.

Ms. Richa Goyal

PATA Award Winner

A young travel and tourism entrepreneur, Richa Goyal received the Faces of the future' award at the 51st Pacific Asia Travel Association's Annual Conference held at New Delhi in January 2002. She was among the 12 young travel professionals selected worldwide. Ms.goyal is part of the top management team of one of the largest wholesale airline and tourism marketing company.

Conclusion

Even if the women have barriers in the society such as look for the family, discrimination in sex, they overlook the barriers and stand in the field of entrepreneurship and help the development of the society and improvement of our country. Many women entrepreneurs encounter the problem and equally compete with men and gets success in the field of entrepreneurship. In modern days, women occupy great role in our country and exceed in commercial growth and economical growth. Hence women entrepreneurship have unique place in development of the society in our country.

TOURISM DEVELOPMENT IN YELAGIRI HILLS

Introduction

Tourism today is one of the most booming sectors in many countries economy. By the year 2006, tourism will be the biggest industry in the world with 850 million tourists, each year. Tourism creates a host of multifarious downstream activities, which have the capacity to substantially involve a large number of people. Apart from generating income, being a labour intensive sector, it generates employment-mostly self-Employment and promoting the over all development of the Tourist destinations. Further more, with the increase in international Tourism, the host country is in a position to earn valuable foreign exchange.

Concept of Tourism

'Tourism may be said to encompass activities pertaining to visit of tourists both domestic and Foreign. Tourism arises from the movement of people to and their study in different destinations.

Tourism is the worlds second largest industry coming next to oil and petroleum industry. Tourism is an industry with out chimneys.

Indian tourism industry, both domestic and foreign, promises to be the major industry of the 21st century. It is likely to get it's legitimate position in the coming years. As on today, it accounts for 50% of the GDP.

Presently India has around 2.5 million tourists a year, placing at 46th in international visitor arrivals of the world Tourism organization (WTO). Thailand and Indonesia have four to five times the number of tourists compares to India and China, which opened its borders a decade ago, has 50 million visitors annually. World tourism is a 350 billion-dollar industry, with every 10th human being a traveler.

Tourism involves

1. Industry with out smoke.
2. Education with out classrooms.
3. Integration with out legislation.
4. Diplomacy with out formality.

Today tourism is also one of the world's fastest growing industries. It earns over $ 3.5 trillion world wide, generated by over 500 million international travelers rising to 850 m by 2006. Even though it has probably the world's highest potential, India's share continues to be 0.37% and the receipts are 0.51% of the world receipts.

Tourism is presently India's 3rd largest export industry after gem jewelry and Readymade garments. The foreign exchange earnings from tourism during 2001-02 was Rs. 104.18b. During the same period 1.4 million tourists arrived in India and over 100 million domestic tourists visited different parts of the country enjoying the diverse cultural heritage of India.

The significant feature of tourism industry is that it employs a large number of women-educated, uneducated, skilled or unskilled persons. It generates employment opportunities particularly in remote and backward areas and it has significant contribution to national integration.

In 2001, about 2 crore people were employed directly and indirectly in this sector.

Tourism is a major contributor to the foreign exchange earnings of several developing and developed countries.

In India, tourism has been recognized as an economic activity especially after the IV five year plan. Tourism forms an important segment of Indian economy in terms of its contribution towards foreign exchange earnings and creation of employment opportunities. The country has a meager share of 0.4% of the world tourist arrivals.

Although India has all the essential ingredients to become major global tourists destinations the inflow of tourists, at 2.34 million in 2001-02 is insignificant constituting just about of 0.36% of global tourists traffic.

Agricultural, industrial and tourism developments are the three ways to bring money and business in to a given region. Tourism development is probably the quickest method of these three. For centuries our people traveled, to know each other, to buy and sell goods, to attend trade fairs and exhibitions and to do research etc.

Tourism is directly linked with the global economic output. According to the recent indicators, the world Gross Domestic Product (GDP) should grow by 3.4% per year over the next decade. Tourist's arrivals into India have grown at a compound rate of 6% in the last ten years compared to the world average of 3%.

Madanlalkhurana former tourism minister said, "The draft of the national policy on tourism which recognizes the role of the central govt., public sector under takings and the private sector in the development of tourism would be reviewed to make it more meaning full".

India has all the essential ingredients. Tourism earned for the country foreign exchange worth Rs. 7,366 crore in 1997-98 registering the single largest item of foreign exchange earner in net terms. During the 9th and 10th plan periods several policy initiatives such as the formation of tourism

Finance Corporation and national action plan were taken to develop the tourism sector.

Tourism touches every one's life. Therefore, the list of things to do may be never ending. But the most important thing is to make a beginning.

Profile of Yelagiri Hills

The tiny hill resort of Vellore Dist. that is Yelagiris is in no way less important to any other renowned hill-resort.

It is actually a poor man's Ooty, Dargiling, Smila, Kodikanal etc.,. But it is grateful to not though the above mentioned other hill resorts are not maintaining their virgin duty due to all round men's havoc in ruining the nature is not here. It is still preserving its virgin duty. But without detrimental to the nature, there is a scope for developing this hill resort. So the step motherly treatment should be put an end to and all round help should be given what it deserves.

Location

Yelagiri Hills is located in Jolarpet panchayat Union of Tirupattur Taluk in Vellore District. It is 27 km north of Tirupattur Town. Yelagiri Hills is situated at 3500 feet above the Madras sea level. It is gifted with natural scenic beauty, cool and pleasant climate and convenient location.

It is well connected by NH 46 SH Roads, and MDR and Railway line to all-important cities.

- To Bangalore by 145 Km by Road.
- To Chennai by 200 Km by Road.

Jolarpet Railway Junction is 18 km out of that 14 Km is ghat section. Starting from Ponneri upto Yelagiri there are 14 hairs pin bends presenting a panoramic view of vast planes.

The plateau of the hill is like a shallow crater adds to the beauty.

The area of the Yelagiri Hills is about 29.2 sq.km. The number of local families in the Yelagiri Hills is 560, in 14 villages.

Population

The population is 9500 (according to the census) out of which 4350 are male and 5150 are female. Of the total 8900 are literate, of which 4350 are male and 4550 are female.

Education

There are four schools. There is one govt. high School and other three higher Secondary schools. The later Higher Secondary Schools are maintained by private Agencies. The student's population is 9000 (5800 boy's and 3200 are girls student) There are 150 Teachers. Of which 90 are male and 60 are female Teachers. The schools have noon meal organizers and Ayahs.

Health

There are three primary Health care centers, and one veterinary center, with normal team of doctors and nurses.

Occupation

The main occupation of the locals is Agriculture to 75%. The remaining 25% are engaged in various other activities related to agriculture and other works like construction and other such small ventures.

Water Supply

There are four protected water supply tanks and five bore wells meeting the need of the villages. There is enough drinking water to the people. There is no water scarcity.

Temples

There are four govt. administered temples namely, Mariyammal, Pungannasiyammal, Perumalappan, and Kathavaniasiyammal.

Food and Commercial Crops

The main food crops are paddy, ragi, cumbu, cholam, samai, which are cultivated on the hills. The main commercial crops are sugar cane and coconut.

Transport

There are enough bus facilities to and fro from important towns to parts of this hill. These are run by govt. and private agencies.

Roads

Black topped roads were laid from 1975 and now then roads are serving all villages.

Climate and Rainfall

The temperature ranges in summer season to 34° and in winter season to 11 mostly the climate is salubrious. The average rainfall here is 900mm per year. The rainy season is from June to December. Cool months are from November to February, Hot months are from March to May.

Ration Shops

There are five govt. run ration shops located at different villages.

Land

There are 1500 acres of land on the plateau of which 1000 are wet-lands and 500 are dry lands. Both electrical and diesel motors are under use.

Bank

State Bank of India has a branch, which gives loans to the farmers for agricultural, and allied activities.

Panchayat Officer

There is one panchayat office at Authanavoor. Govt. built community halls for each village are there.

Post Office

There is a head post office at Authanavoor and sub-post offices at Punganoor and Kottioour all in govt. buildings.

Electricity

There are six transformers at

Authanavoor:	2
Punguanor:	1
Nilavur:	1
Mangalam :	1
Kottiour :	1

Lakes

There are four lakes at Athanavoor, Mangalam, Punguanor and Nilavur. In the Punguanoor Lake boating facility is available. All the four lakes have water through out the year. Around 1000 acres of lands are irrigated.

Tourist Placaes in Yelagiri Hills

(a) Punguanoor Lake and Garden

Sufficient number of rowing and pedal boats are available.

A newly laid flori culture garden is adding to the beauty.

(b) Paran – "A Hanging View Point"

One gets a panoramic view of the plaints giving the impression of being around hanging gardens of babylonia.

(c) Heritage Village of India

In Nilavur village around the "Thambiran lotus pond" a Heritage village exits exhibiting our Indian rural culture and how it contributes to the modern India.

(d) Other Places of Interest

(i) Poly green house (Lack Side).

(ii) Sericulture farm (Mangalam Village).

(iii) Mangalam fishing pond.

(iv) Nachiamman koil.

(v) Murugan koil and valley view point.

(vi) Thayalur Horticulture farm (YMCA boy's camp).

(vii) Telescope House.

Trekking Routes

This small and beautiful hill station offers good opportunity for trekking and mountaineering. It is endowed with several trekking routes through the dense reserved forests measuring from 1 Km to 5 Kms.

Sami Malai

Sami malai and jalakampari areas have such trekking routes. The peak point of the routs is samimalai hills, which is 4338 feet above mean sea level.

Summer Festivals

The Govt. conducts summer festivals, during May-June, for three days. During the summer festivals in various programmes are conducted by the Govt. as well as by private agencies.

Programmes During Summer Festivals

1. Entertainment programmes.

2. Exhibitions.
3. Culture Programmes.
4. Awareness Programmes by the Govt departments.

Local Festivals

(i) Nachiamman temple festival in Nilavur once in five years.

(ii) Murugan temple festival every year.

Suggestions

The author suggests the following not by way of complaints, but by way of adding to the present conditions in developing this into a better resort.

Along the trekking route, the forest department should identify the botanical names of the trees sharubus and herbs and grasses. For the trekkers, a forest guide to follow the trekkers. The trekkers, if they are college students, especially botany or zoology will be grateful to collect herbarium specimens. So the govt. should permit this and also to permit to carry with them vasculam. This will spread the name and fame lot of this resort. The guide should be in a position to appraise the trekers as to the safety of wild life. In the trekking roads, there should be watering facility land resting facility plus toilet facility. At the beginning of the trekking route, there should be a library with books of the available botanical and zoological items.

There should be films on wild life forestry etc,. There should be cassettes to department. The department should take steps to provide more fodder for the wild life. There must be a sanctun sanctorium and the trekkers should be helped with binoculars to look at the wild life within the sanctun sanctorium. The trekkers should be made to plant saplings at least one each.

There should be dormitory for groups of youngsters to rest at a very nominal so cost. There should be information centers on the times of Thirupathi Devasthanam at Madras, Vellore, Tirupattur, Vaniyambadi, Ponneri etc. places. There should also be slides. These are the few suggestions. I wish that this hill resort to prosper all round.

Biblography

Tourism: "10th Five Year Plan", Vol. II, Govt. of India Planning Commission, New Delhi, 2002-2007, p. 925.

Pranseth (2004), "Successful Tourism Management", Vol. I, Sterling Publishers Private Ltd., pp. 82 to 96.

Pranseth (1977), "Successful Tourism Management", Vol. I, Sterling Publishers Private Ltd, pp. 80 to 91.

Jayant Joshi (1973), "Tourist Diary", pp. 33 to 178.

S.A. Alagarsamy (2003), "Tamil Nadu Many Attractions for a Tourist", Yojana Augutst, pp. 79 to 80.

Tourism (2004), "10th Five Year Plan", Tamil Nadu 2002-2007, State Planning Commission, July, pp. 307 to 311.

S.A. Alagarsamy (2002), "Tamil Nadu Many Attraction for Tourist", Yojana. Aug, p. 79,80.

Towards Better Tourism Development (2004), "Urban Development and Tourism", Vol II, p.143.

Prasenth (2004), "Successful Tourism Management", Vol. I, Sterling Publishers Private Ltd, New Delhi, pp. 125, 126.

A. Vijaya Kumar (2003), "New Strategy for Indian Tourism Industry", Southern Economist, 1st Oct. p. 18, 19.

WOMEN EMPOWERMENT THROUGH SELF HELP GROUPS

Introduction

A Self Help Group is voluntary group valuing personal interaction and mutual laid as a means of altering and ameliorating problems perceived as alterable, pressing and personal by most of its participants. The Self Help Group has been utilized in a growing number of projects and programmes. The characteristic features of self help groups includes:

- Voluntary membership
- Participatory Planning
- Education and training
- Resource mobilization
- Self management
- Anti bureaucracy
- Empowerment building
- Process extension & movement building
- On going evaluation
- Sustainability

Self help group takes different forms in different countries according to the needs of local groups. SHG concept has gained momentum now-a-days. And its routes have penetrated in almost all villages in Tamil Nadu.

Women's Movement

Throughout history, women have collectively struggled against direct and indirect barriers to their self-development. By the end of 19th century, they have begun to organize themselves. Gradually they look up a number of causes such as education, conditions of women's work and so on. At present women's movement focuses on equality and empowerment. The activism within the women movement has influenced policy and planning of the government and development of empowerment.

Workingwomen can be classified into different categories as:

- Women Entrepreneurs
- Highly qualified professionals
- Employees in organized public and private sector and others

Self Help Group

The most important social innovation to help the poor in recent years has been the success of thrift and credit based self help groups especially these formed by women. These groups have successfully development a system of revolving credit for the benefit of group members based on their own savings. Linking of SHGs to formal financial institutions has further enhanced availability of micro credit financing to the groups. SHGs have successfully maintained a high rate of loan repayments and generated additional income, jobs and small enterprises for their members.

Concept of Women Empowerment

Women empowerment concept was introduced at the international women's conference in 1985 at Nairobi. It aimed at enhancing their social functioning by a quantitative and qualitative change particularly in the field of education, health and employment, which will bring the desired level of change. The Government and voluntary organizations are providing many income generating schemes to raise the economic status of women.

By realizing the importance of SHGs, the governments, banks and NGOs are extending their support by providing various schemes. The micro finance programme has made rapid strides in India with a loan portfolio of Rs. 2048.676 crores on March 31, 2003. The program has enabled the formal banking system to reach the doorsteps of 116 lakh poor households through 7.17 lakh SHGs.

Working Pattern of SHGs

- SHGs collect deposits from their members and lend to the needy members for production purposes and for subsistence and consumption needs.
- They take loans from banks to meet the needs of the members.
- Assess individual credit needs of members and submit to the bank for sanction of collective loans.
- NGO helps the SHGs in procuring raw materials and marketing of the produce.
- Collectively ensuring the repayment of bank loans.
- Entire loan amount disbursed to SHGs is refinanced by NABARD to the financing bank.

Capacity for Women's Development

Assisting SHGs establish a track record of sound credit management based on their own savings and strengthen the capacity to support agencies, such as state level women's development corporation, NGO's banks, and line departments to provide them with better service.

Mechanisms to access social programs and leverage funds for creation of community assets

The project will assist communities to create needed assets such as drinking water facilities, sanitation, multi-purpose halts/day care centers, or acquiring teaching/learning materials, thus improving women's access to social services such as health, child care, and education. This project will also help to leverage contributions from ongoing government programs for community development activities. By the end of the project it is expected that the self help group formed will have sufficient literacy among their members to function smoothly.

Achievement through SHGs

In this way synergy of progress can be achieved:

- As women receive grated education and training, they will earn more money.
- As women earn more money, they spend it in the further education and health of their children.
- As women rise in economic status, they will gain greater social standing in the household and the village, and will have greater voice.
- They will make stronger claims to their entitlements gaining further training better access to credit and higher incomes and command attention of police and courts when attacked.
- It will be easy to overcome the tradition of "Son preference" and thus put an end to the evil of dowry.
- Age of marriage rises.
- 20 per cent of child death drops and wages rise by 10 per cent.
- As women are better nourished and marry later, they will be healthier, more productive and will give birth to healthier babies.

Conclusion

"Woman is the companion of man, gifted with equal mental capacities. She has the right to participate in minute at details of activities of man and she has the same right of freedom and liberty as he/she is entitled to a supreme place in her own sphere of activity as man is in his'

—Mahatma Gandhi

"Gender equality is more than a goal itself. It is a precondition for meeting the challenge of reducing poverty, promoting sustainable development and building good governance' says the **UNO Secretary General, Kofi Annan.**

This recognition is currently missing in India. Transforming the prevailing social discrimination against women must become the top priority, and must happen concurrently with increased direct action to rapidly improve the social and economic status of women.

References

SHGs–A movement for Women Empowerment–Department of Agricultural extension & Rural Sociology, Agricultural College and Research Institute, TNAU, Madurai.

Websites

www.bambooweb.com

www.shg.co.in